FEELS LIKE
REDEMPTION

Praise for Seth Taylor

"I have enormous respect for Seth Taylor. He lives the integrity that we need for the way forward today."

Author of Echo of the Soul: The Sacredness of the Human Body, A New Harmony, and The Rebirthing of God: Christianity's Struggle for New Beginnings

"In *Feels Like Redemption*, Seth Taylor offers us the gift of his own untidy, yet glorious journey toward real freedom, vitality, and life. If you've ever wondered whether Christianity has more to offer your soul than what you've known so far, this book will rock your world."

—*Michael John Cusick*
Author of Surfing for God: Discovering the Divine Desire Beneath Sexual Struggle

"Seth takes the wisdom of the practice of pilgrimage and uses it as a redemptive lens for an often taboo topic in the Church, reminding readers that healing is not a quick fix, but a journey, and that faith is not about perfection, but ongoing transformation."

—*Lacy Clark Ellman*
Spiritual Director and Author of Pilgrim Principles: Journeying with Intention in Everyday Life

"Lots of people write about liberation, Seth has lived it. Seth Taylor is the real deal."

—*Rob Bell*
Author of *What We Talk About When We Talk About God, Love Wins,* and *Sex God: Exploring the Endless Connections Between Sexuality and Spirituality*

"Seth Taylor is courageously entering into a conversation about a topic most of us simply avoid. In this book he doesn't demand you embrace or even follow his path to healing, he simply challenges his reader to think and feel honestly , and to look back with introspection and without shame."

—*Ron Ruthruff*
Associate Professor of Theology and Culture at The Seattle School of Theology and Psychology and Author of The Least of These: Lessons Learned from Kids on the Street

"I've known Seth for a few years and I've been privileged to watch his Pilgrimage from up close. I believe in his story as it offers hope that freedom is always possible"

—*Steve Zakuani*
Professional Soccer Player and Author of the upcoming book 500 Days

"Seth proves himself a trustworthy conversation partner for a difficult journey. *Feels Like Redemption* isn't just about pornography or addiction, its a story of coming alive again to the good desires God has given us, and how the road to wholeness is more complicated, beautiful, and honest than any self-help book or theology of instant fixes. If you're looking for life, not just guilt-driven self-control, then I dare you to walk this pilgrimage with Seth."

—*Morgan Schmidt*
Youth Pastor & Author of Woo: Awakening Teenagers' Desire to Follow in the Way of Jesus

"*Feels like Redemption* is a field guide to walking the terrain of addiction. Seth invites us to face how much of our pack is filled with extraneous paraphernalia from not facing our story and not reading the Bible well. This disruptive book demands a new reading of the illusions related to how we find life and offers the immense promise that facing our heartache also offers the mystery of joy."

—*Dan B. Allender Ph.D*
Professor of Counseling Psychology at and founding President of The Seattle School of Theology and Psychology and Author of God Loves Sex: An Honest Conversation about Sexual Desire and Holiness and Intimate Allies: Rediscovering God's Design for Marriage and Becoming Soul Mates for Life

FEELS LIKE REDEMPTION

The pilgrimage to health and healing

SETH TAYLOR
with DAVID GLENN TAYLOR

FOREWORD BY CRAIG GROSS

Published in Los Angeles, CA, by Fireproof Ministries Inc. Fireproof Ministries Inc., titles may be purchased in bulk for educational, business, fund-raising, or sales promotional use. For information, please e-mail info@fireproofministries.com.

Unless otherwise noted, Scriptures are taken from the Holy Bible, New International Version®,NIV®. Copyright © 1973, 1978, 1984, 2011 by Biblica, Inc.™ Used by permission of Zondervan. All rights reserved worldwide. www.zondervan.com.

Scriptures marked nkjv are from THE NEW KING JAMES VERSION.
© 1982 by Thomas Nelson, Inc. Used by permission. All rights reserved.

The Library of Congress Cataloging-in-Publication
Data is on file with the Library of Congress
ISBN-13: 978-0692217351

For Floyd, Marianne, and Monty
For showing us the path

TABLE OF CONTENTS

FOREWORD

I made some new friends, Seth and David Taylor, because of this book. My name is Craig Gross, and I run a ministry called XXXchurch which is dedicated to people who deal with porn. Whether they make it or use it, we provide them with resources to help them stop either one. One of those resources is a software product called X3watch that helps decrease their porn use and start using the internet in healthy, life-giving ways.

So you can imagine my interest when I heard about the interesting personal experiences Seth and Dave have had with pornography and finding freedom from it; they share those in this book, which was brought to my attention through a mutual friend. I read it, and decided I had to let people know about this additional method of finding freedom.

In the book, Seth writes about a treatment center in Alaska that his brother Dave visited, a place where Dave learned some spiritual practices that sounded a little new to me, but that helped him. Seth ended up heading to Alaska after hearing his brother rave about this, and subsequently was delivered of his porn addiction.

The book itself is not about Alaska (not really, anyway), but after a conference call with Seth and his brother talking about the book, the design, the roll-out of a companion video series, and all those things, they asked me to come to Alaska and check it out.

I agreed.

For those who know me, it shouldn't surprise you: I'm always up for something new and always want to see something firsthand before I draw my conclusions about it.

But I didn't want to go alone, so I invited a few friends to come with me. I didn't want people just like me, but I needed people open to something new. A lot of times Christians (which I am) are close-minded and push away anything out of the box.

Oftentimes our favorite speaker or pastor says one thing we disagree with and we discredit everything they ever have said. Jay Bakker came out in support of gays and lost a ton of support and followers. Rob Bell questioned hell and made a lot of people discredit all his other teachings.

I hate buffets and would never eat at one by choice, but when it comes to my faith I am wide open to a collection of teachers and thoughts that shape my understanding of the scriptures. Now, I'm still limited in my taste; I am not going to pull truths from Scientology or Mormonism, but I enjoy bits and pieces of a number of different Christian speakers and teachers from a range of different set of beliefs from within Christianity.

I wanted people like *that* with me. So, I invited... Ryan. One of my best friends for 20 years and a partner in ministry with me for the last 6 years. Recently divorced and a former pastor who is by far the person most similar to me in personality as anyone I have ever met.

Sam. A creative friend of mine whom I have known for 8 years. He had a crazy couple of years on and off drugs and alcohol, and is now wide open in terms of his belief system.

Dave. A performer friend of 15 years. He's a creative musician who is always up for anything and will do it 100%. Recently divorced and not sure what he believes after years of belonging to a strict evangelical church culture.

We had no idea what would happen, but we were open to anything. Good thing, because our expectations were upended when we arrived at the center at 5 pm on Friday in Anchorage, Alaska. We thought we'd be heading to a hotel or office building or conference center; what we found instead was a residential neighborhood in the middle of town.

This wasn't a treatment center—it was someone's house.

The house belonged to Floyd and Marianne, the married couple who facilitate treatment, and it was indeed the right place. Marianne came outside to greet us and show us to the area where we would be resting. Since I wrote the check for the four of us, I was the only one out of the 25 people attending that weekend's session who was lucky enough to get my own room. The other three guys got a room together; everyone else just slept on mats on the floor.

Soon everyone had arrived and, after handing over our shoes into their custody, we were told we couldn't leave the house until Sunday night. That raised some alarm bells for me, but I quieted them and tried my hardest to participate when we did some tribal chant and made a verbal commitment that what was said there would stay there.

Now I was really wondering what I'd gotten into. And what would they think of the video cameras we'd brought with us?

Come on. You didn't think I was going to fly to Alaska with three of my friends, get locked in some house for two straight days, and *not* shoot video footage of it?

I had no plans on what to *do* with any footage we got, but just knew we needed to record everything we had permission to record, so we put our two Canon 7Ds and three GoPros to work. We shot the general check-in sessions and the meals, but were only allowed to shoot the core emotional processes for us four, plus Seth's and one other female attendee who allowed us.

The first session Friday night was a check-in. This is where we all sat in a circle and everyone shared what led them to Alaska and what they were hoping to get out of the weekend.

It lasted three and a half hours.

Then we broke up into five different rooms so Marianne and Floyd could identify, based on our check-in, who was ready to "be processed." No surprise: neither Ryan nor I was "ready," but Dave was, so off he went, our cameras in tow.

What happened during the process? Everyone split up into groups of 4-5 participants and one leader, all in different rooms all over the house. (By the way, I don't know why they call it "processing," but that's their term, so that's what I will use.) The first person lies down on a mat (think: gymnastics mat or cheap bed mattress on the ground). The leader (in our case either Marianne or Floyd) places a blindfold over their eyes and covers them with a blanket.

This is what Marianne did with Dave and then, since all four of us (mostly) believe in Jesus and the Holy Spirit, one of us (I don't remember who) offered up a short prayer for him:

"Dear Lord, we pray for this time. We thank you for Dave and pray right now that your spirit would reveal itself to Dave and be with him now."

Marianne asked Dave to start breathing in slow, deep breaths, exhaling from his core. Then she asked a few questions based on an intake survey he'd done, while the rest of us listened. After the process is finished (which: that's decided when the person just decides they're done and takes off the blindfold), something powerful happens. Each person there speaks into your life based on what they just witnessed. There are more tears at times, encouragement, and some incredible moments as you just sit and be present with someone and hear their story.

Dave's process was highly emotional, but then again, so is Dave. As he progressed, he was able to let go of some anger that he had been holding onto for years. His process lasted about an hour or so, but it can take up to 2 or 3 hours (or longer) for others. I wondered how long mine would last.

When we finished, I spent a few minutes wandering throughout the house on my way to my room and listened to some of the other processes in progress. I heard screaming, crying, yelling, punching, bat-swinging, anger and just about every emotion possible. Part of me didn't know what I was getting myself into, but of course I wanted to "be ready" to give it a go the next day.

I finally went to bed Saturday morning at 4:00, excited to see what might surface during my processing. Less than six hours later, I was awakened by a knock on my door.

I was told to eat breakfast quickly and then get ready—we were doing another check-in. At this point, I was starting to lose my open-minded, I'm-up-for-anything attitude and was thinking more about how great sleeping feels. But, I got up and headed over for another round of check-in.

I'll be honest—I consider myself a nice guy, and I love helping people, but I have very little patience for listening to people talk about themselves, especially in this kind of setting. I wasn't all that enthused for another round of this, and my enthusiasm took a nose dive when we had to do two exercises: a Hawaiian chant and then looking into one another's eyes and saying, "You are the beloved." After that, we had to go around the circle and listen in depth while everyone talked about how the exercises made us feel.

Ryan: no comment

Me: the beloved part was awkward and the chant was worse than singing bad worship songs.

Dave: loved the chant and wanted to sing it to his kids when he got home

Sam: I actually can't tell you what Sam said, because by the time we got around the circle to him, it was 3 hours later and I was too bothered and bored to pay attention.

Look, this chanting and touchy-feely stuff is fine and good for some people, and if that sort of thing works for you, I'm really happy for you. But this was not what I thought I was getting into—I was more interested in the processing, not the check-in, but the processing seemed to get farther and farther away from me.

But then it happened. Marianne told me that I would get to do the processing soon. Sam first, then Ryan, then me.

Finally.

I've tried yoga twice; I hated it because I am not flexible and I don't like sitting in a room on a mat. I like scoring points, making goals, and beating someone at something. Though I have several counselor friends, I've only been to a counselor once. I've spent a total of two months—ever—in a church small group. I run pretty fast in general, but last year I started getting crippling headaches, which led me to slow down and work on the book *Go Small*

This was all in my head as I prepared for the process. I had traveled 3000 miles to Alaska with an open mind, and all my sarcasm, criticism, and critique of the whole weekend wound up doing nothing to dent the experience of my process. I've been alive for 38 years and been a Christian for 32 of those, and I've never experienced anything like this.

Quick diversion: I have a friend named Matt who loves to tell stories and share stories and listen to stories. Matt was on the board of our ministry—all of us guys and all of us friends—and about eight years ago we had a board meeting weekend in Philadelphia. Matt suggested that, instead of a normal meeting, each guy would share his story.

What story? Think of your life as a movie, but you only have about 1 hour to share the highs and lows. Then people around the room ask questions.

We did it as a board and it was great. I did it later with a group of friends in Michigan, along with our wives and three of our couple friends, and on a few other occasions with our staff over the last 8 years. If you have never done that with your friends or family... its the only thing better than Cards Against Humanity, and a great bonding and growing experience.

So I anticipated that processing was simply going to be a next-level version of this, but with a little more focus on the pain instead of the joys. When you share your story in a group of friends, you try to be honest, but you tell things from your point of view and oftentimes skip the really hard stuff in exchange for the good things.

Processing was not that.

Before we began, we reminded Marianne why we'd come in the first place. For me, it was because I'd had headaches for a year. For Sam, it was not being able to sleep after coming off drugs. For Ryan, it was experiencing peace in his life after divorce. For Seth and his brother Dave, it was their struggles with pornography.

I can't speak to each of those guys' experiences exactly, but I can tell you about mine. First, the breathing. When you're lying down on your back with a blindfold on, just staring into blackness, something happens. I breathed so heavily that I raised my heartbeat; not really like a workout, but still so intense that my mind cleared enough where I could think of nothing beyond my next breath.

Let's pause for a second. I wrote a book called *Go Small* with my friend Adam Palmer. We talked about slowing down and moving out of the way, but let's be honest: this is really hard. How many times during the day can you just shut your mind off? Can you just stare into space and lose track of time and your commitments or challenges and just check out? It's hard... really hard.

In the midst of this, with nothing happening but breathing and darkness and time slowing down, Marianne asked me to think about my childhood.

"What image do you see?"

Clear as day I saw a Porsche 911 my dad had when I was very young. He owned a Sizzler restaurant and drove this cool car. I remember riding in it one day after he got into a fight with my mom, and that's the moment that came to my mind during processing.

I only worried about two things my whole childhood:

1. My parents getting a divorce
2. My house getting robbed.

We lived in Stockton, California for a while, and our house was hit a few times before we finally got a dog. She kept everyone away, but man, was I scared at night. So that's where that fear came from.

When I was 14, my dad received a large check from his brother with a note that said, "Open your own restaurant." The Sizzler had driven my dad to bankruptcy and that Porsche was long gone. Since then, he'd worked for Chuck E. Cheese's, Burger King, and Long John Silver's, but he'd always wanted his own place again. My mom was against it, and the night that check came, my dad insisted he would use the money for something else.

He bought vending machines instead. In what would become an ironic twist, given my line of work, his first two accounts were the two local strip clubs. One problem, though: they wanted prices changed from .50 cents to $1.00 on all the manual coin operated machines. My dad had no clue how to do it, so he gave the job to me to figure out. And that became my new job. I spent hours and hours and hours fixing vending machines as a kid. Why? Fear. Fear that, if this business didn't work out, my mom and dad would split up. If that meant leaving school early and going to the strip club before it opened so I could fix a vending machine, then that's what I would do. (To this day, I hate doing any kind of work with my hands around the house. Jeanette fixes everything.) It didn't last. After 40 years, my parents separated in 2011 when I was 35 years old. And this all came out in the darkness on the mat. And then, suddenly, I became aware of my son Nolan, who has two fears in his life:

1. Our house being broken into again (because we were hit one time within 3 months of moving in)

2. Jeanette and I splitting up (he is so aware every time we have a fight and seems overly concerned our marriage might end).

While this was in my mind, Marianne asked me about my headaches. I have prayed that they go away. I have asked God for a sign and have had every test in the book, including 2 MRIs, CAT scans, a seizure test, MS screening, spinal tap… and though I've asked tons of doctors why I had these headaches, *I never asked God.*

Isn't it interesting that we ask God for things all the time? That we say *what* a lot more than *why*? We want the *what*, but maybe the *what* is really in the *why*.

"Why don't you ask God why you get headaches?" Marianne asked.

So I did. Then a loud voice came down from heaven, and the earth shook, and the answer was written in the sky.

Not really.

But after a few minutes, another image came to my mind. You may call it random, but laying on a mat blindfolded for an hour and a half, I felt it was just me and God there, with me truly listening and trying to experience him rather than talk to him.

That is a key thing I learned here. For years, I have talked to God. A very few times in my life, I have heard his voice, clearly audible, and made decisions based on that, but here I learned that part of the process is the ability to just sit, be present and listen, and try to experience his spirit.

Anyway, the image: it was the summer of 1987. I was at skateboard camp at UC Santa Cruz, in a dorm room, looking at a *Playboy* centerfold hanging on the wall, with a sticker for the skateboard wheels company Slimeballs cleverly covering the model's crotch.

I immediately gathered two things this image might tell me:

1. I have headaches because of a struggle with porn.

2. I have headaches because of the ministry of XXX-church.com I run and have given 13 years of my life to.

I don't really feel that I am involved in a struggle with porn (I don't ever use it and have never been addicted), so I quickly ditched #1 and leaned into #2 and that scared me. Maybe I needed to find some better balances and slow down? Maybe I needed to step down from that ministry and throw in the towel? I didn't know, but it got me wondering and more aware.

I thought my processing time was up, and was grateful for the image because it gave me something to think about, when Ryan said something I don't think I will ever forget. He said "Craig, I was with you this past year in some groundbreaking times of your life. The night you found out your dad had passed away, the night I drove you to the ER thinking you were dying in Arizona, and one other night where you and I laughed like we have never have before in our lives." He then went on to ask me about the extreme highs and lows he saw me encounter, and we had a blindfolded conversation.

Now, Ryan as you read this, don't think I'm saying you're an angel, because you're not. But there was something beautiful here. I've spent years attending church and hearing, "Where two or more are gathered, I am there." Church folks try and convince us that when we gather and listen to some sermon with 100-plus other people, God is there. But maybe that verse really means there's a depth you just don't see when you stare at the backs of people's heads in a church service.

The Lord's presence was there in that room during my processing, and I believe he was speaking through Ryan at that very moment. But to explain my next breakthrough, I have to tell you one more thing about my dad.

For some reason, my dad was convinced he wouldn't die until he was 87, so when he got sick at age 70, I just figured he would pull through. We weren't close while I was growing up, but we'd reconnected when I was 31 and had an amazing relationship. I didn't want him to go, and I miss him dearly.

I've grieved his passing. I've cried more about losing my dad than anything else in my life. Many nights I sit in a Jacuzzi I bought with money he left me and just talk to my dad and cry. I think I've handled it okay, but then again I have only lost three people that were close to me in my life so maybe I don't know how to deal with death.

Laying on that mat and talking to Ryan, I suddenly realized that my dad's death did something to me: it rattled me to the point of fear for my own life. Sure, I got sick after his death and have had real symptoms, but I've flown a million miles in the past 15 years. I'm on flights all the time, yet after my father's death, I've been terrified to fly. Every time I fly, I suffer an extreme sense of panic and fear and I can't shake it.

I'm terrified of leaving my kids and my wife like my dad left me. The thought has consumed me and has almost paralyzed me.

That's what I needed to deal with.

Once I knew that, I sat up, got off the mat, and listened while my friends said a few things to me that were really powerful (and which will remain with me).

But even so, it was just too much to take in all at once. I left the room with my head spinning with all the thoughts, consequences, and ways these realizations could wind up playing out in the real world.

Now you can understand why I was ready to leave the center the next morning. Unfortunately, *they* weren't ready for it.

Sunday morning. Ryan and I got ready to take off from the treatment center so we could contemplate our processing—and so we could get our freedom back. We ate breakfast (a great meal!) and called a taxi; 20 minutes later, the car was in the driveway.

We packed our bags in the meantime (and found our shoes) and told Seth and Marianne we were taking off. Dave and Sam were still asleep, and they were more into it than we were; Sam may have wanted to leave if the flight-change fee wasn't $200, but Dave was actually enjoying the whole thing. Regardless, they were staying.

The staff at the Center were less than thrilled we decided to leave early. Marianne told us all we would be missing (more check-ins, more chanting, etc.) none of which compared to seeing my kids and Jeanette one day sooner—especially after my processing revelations—so we left.

Once we were in the cab, Ryan and I got out the GoPro and recorded our entire conversation on the drive to the airport; once we arrived there, we sat and talked for two hours while waiting for my flight out (Ryan stayed behind to go backpacking in the Alaskan wilderness). We just laughed about everything and took guesses on when Sam and Dave would actually be done (they were still there through Sunday night).

I'm glad I went.

I would never go back.

Even though 90 percent of the weekend was painful and pretty weird, the time we spent processing and watching our friends process was incredibly transformational and life-changing.

I had a lot on my mind the morning after processing, and that has led me to keep making sense of all this information and these thoughts. But remember the panic I had when it came to flying? I can't explain what I felt walking onto that first flight out of Alaska. It was the opposite of panic. It truly was a peace that passed all understanding.

I didn't ask for that. I didn't expect that. I just got it. Maybe I let that fear go on the mat. Maybe I was able to let it go because I had finally figured out what I needed to let go of.

My second flight was a puddle-jumper from San Francisco to Burbank; recently, I would rather have driven seven hours than get on that flight, but this time: peace. Among the turbulence, I sat and cranked out work like the good old days of flying.

Maybe this was a summer-camp-high experience! Right? Maybe the fear would creep back in and paralyze me again. Well, right now I'm writing this while headed to Portland and I'm not lying when I tell you I have the same peace.

I don't have any concrete things to tell you about my headaches and health — it's too soon — but I will share when I learn more. In the meantime, I said something else on the mat that I haven't mentioned yet. I was scared to do it, but I realized I needed to do it.

My dad was a die-hard fan of the San Francisco 49ers. Our last trip together was to Candlestick Park to see his 49ers crush my Green Bay Packers in 2013 playoffs. He died 3 weeks later. He had season tickets as a kid to the 49ers prior to them being at Candlestick, and then again when they moved to Candlestick.

The 49ers now have a new stadium; my dad and I had talked about going to it together once it opened. He didn't live to see them play in the new place, but I did. So I took my friend David Dean and went to the opening game in that new facility, and you know what? It was great. It was hard, but great. My old self would've run from something like that because of the pain and loss associated, but I decided I needed to go and be there.

Because that's what my dad and I were going to do. I can't wait to tell him about the new stadium one day.

So, what about you? Do you need to experience freedom from something? Do you need to let go of something that has taken control of your life? Do you need to break free from an addiction? You can do it.

What you are about to read is going to help you. Finding freedom is not a battle, but rather it is a journey. This book and the guidebook that accompanies it will point you down a possible path you can use to go on that journey. They're going to push you to process some of these things and start asking the question why and start feeling. It will be uncomfortable at times, and maybe even painful, but trust me: we are not asking you to lie down with a blindfold in the middle of Alaska. My trip to Alaska simply opened my eyes to some thoughts and practices I had never tried nor known much about.

Getting to know Seth and David has been even more of an eye opener to see people truly break free of their addictions. Even Ryan has started integrating some of the things he learned in this book and in Alaska and has finally found the peace that he couldn't find for years, and Sam has slept like a baby every night since he got back.

I don't know what you are looking for or why you picked up this book but my prayer is that, as you read it and step out on this pilgrimage, you realize that freedom is possible.

— Craig Gross, November 2014

STARTING WITH THE ENDING

Several years ago, something happened to my brother that started a chain reaction of radical healing and transformation in my life. At that point, I had been a porn addict for about seven years, my marriage was dying, if not already dead, and I was burdened by such heavy depression and anxiety that I had begun to wonder whether life was worth living anymore. I tried many of the prescribed methods of recovery, including reading popular books, but the methods those books taught seemed to say true freedom wasn't really possible. It seemed the best I could hope for was to control my addiction and survive my depression and anxiety with various coping methods.

It wasn't until my twin brother Dave tried a radical form of therapy in Alaska, where he lives, that I began to find the freedom I desired, a freedom I could physically *feel*. Dave will tell a bit about his process of discovery later on, but I found that what happened to him became easily adaptable within my own life. I didn't need a guided tour through my mind in a house in Alaska; I just needed a quiet place and a few principles to apply.

This book is about my discovery of real healing, and it anticipates you will have a few questions as to what life looks like on the other side of that type of transformation. So, as much as I cannot tell you what is on your path — every pilgrimage is deeply personal and has its own twists and turns, and your experiences may be radically different from mine — I can certainly start this process by telling you what I've learned in the wake of so much powerful change. Here, in question and answer form, is what my life beyond porn addiction looks like now.

So...you seriously never look at porn anymore?

At first, I felt like Superman. I was literally impervious to any type of addictive or negative sexual stimuli for about six months. I didn't even experience what you might call "temptation" in that time. And it wasn't a religious type of purity — it was more like a feeling that I was indestructible sexually. It was bliss. My addiction was gone, that was for sure, because the pain I had been medicating with porn for so long was gone.

But after those six months, things started to shift. My experience was so disorienting to my understanding of my Christian faith that, in order to keep growing, I enrolled in a graduate program at The Seattle School of Theology and Psychology. I went looking for someone to tell me something I hadn't heard before. I was desperate for something *new*. I found it in the Masters in Theology and Culture program.

This program, along with the other programs offered there, is intensely focused on the intersection of theology and deep inner healing. In other words, I did *a lot* of therapy. As I studied theology, psychology, and philosophy, I was expected to engage my story, and thus my pain, as it pertains to these disciplines. Of course, engaging one's story involves confronting the other questions in one's life. In my case, questions such as, "So, I'm not an addict anymore—what about the depression I'm still suffering from? I can't seem to *do* the things I *want* to do." "What about the anxiety, especially surrounding money? I've always been poor. How do my pain and theology affect that?" "Why do I feel so insecure around my peers?" And so on...

These were serious questions, each one of them rooted in deep pain. It functioned in layers, each of the issues in my life being rooted in wounds I carried at various levels. I now believe each one can be healed. I didn't want to just stop at healing my porn addiction. I wanted to find out what I was created to be, and my spirit was telling me how to get there: keep going inward. So I did.

The downside to this was that each time I encountered something or someone that triggered the deeper wounds, my pain would surface and demand medication. Each time, I would have a choice whether to suppress that pain again or allow myself to feel it.

I know that the language here can be difficult, because technically speaking, *I've always had a choice.* Even as addicts, we have an intellectual understanding that we have a choice... we just don't know what the options are. I came to understand that the options were to either medicate (in my case, use porn) or to do "the work" to process the pain, which for me has come in the form of meditation and prayer.

The difference in my choices, before my transformation and after, is the level of consciousness.

If a person is making their choices while living in an unconscious world, as if they are asleep, shrouded by pain that is itself shrouded in fear, anger, and anxiety, then can it be said they are truly making a choice? How can you make a choice when you can't even see? Addiction is the feeling of having no choice, even though you actually do. There are parts of me that want healing, and parts of me that don't, but in light of the healing I have received over the years, I've found my choices have become clearer and also much, much easier to make.

As I have learned to heal over the years, I often needed and sought out help, as will you, to *move* the pain out of my body and really heal. And since feeling the pain is a part of healing the pain, I learned how to do that on my own, though my twin brother Dave would sometimes catch me in a mental tailspin and pull me out with a, "Dude—take a deep breath and tell me what you're feeling." Sometimes I made the choice to medicate with pornography, but even in those rare moments, I always expected to hold to the curiosity of what I was medicating. What was I trying to recover? The question was (and is) always there: do I want to be transformed? I always have the choice whether I am going to give in to the demands my pain makes or if I will move past that pain and into a deeper experience of con-sciousness...and by *consciousness,* I mean *seeing* God. Either way, there is no shame. I live under the knowledge that God is not angry with me in any way—and this allows me to see more clearly and move forward.

And let me be clear, medicating with pornography is now a very rare occurrence in my life. I will never be able to apply the term addict to my identity ever again. It was important that I came to grips with that word and how it applied to me at one point, but no longer. And I am finding that my sexuality is walking more and more in the light of desire as opposed to some sort of animalistic appetite.

Do you feel guilty when you medicate?

No. Not even a little bit. I know that may sound confus-ing. Many people believe guilt serves a useful purpose for keeping us from doing evil things, as if feeling guilt is the difference between us normal people and sociopaths. Many wives I have spoken with only trust that things will change for their husbands if there is a sufficient amount of guilt present. And those that are Christians often confuse guilt with the conviction of the Holy Spirit. They assume the presence of guilt is synonymous with the presence of motivation for change.

This is not the case.

Our behaviors were meant to be, and are more powerful when, driven by wisdom rooted in the Spirit, not by conviction manifested as shame and guilt. Even as I have continued to dig into deeper pain and find healing for deeper wounds, my shame has never returned, and thus I can see very clearly that wallowing in guilt is completely pointless. In my case, wisdom has replaced guilt. And the grace of God is able to shine brighter in my weakness.

I have also come to believe that the real freedom I will describe in this book isn't a freedom from sin, but rather a freedom from ~~shame~~. Or put a different way, *freedom from shame* is *freedom from sin*. The idea that I am bad is no longer, and will never again be, an operative truth in my life. My spirit has come alive and as a result, the loss of shame has been the most profound change in me. It is a very distinct feeling. It gives me confidence, provides a visceral experience of hope in everyday life, and allows room for happiness in a very authentic way.

That freedom always moves me forward, even when I am in pain. There is no cycle of guilt-shame-repent-repeat anymore.

What does your wife think about all of this?

My marriage was nothing short of a living hell for a long time, so the transformation in that arena is one of the more amazing parts of my story. My wife's perspective on my healing is a valuable one, so I asked her this question, and this is what she said. (She is a therapist, so that might explain some of the language she uses to describe her experience.)

AMY: In the past, I knew when you were using porn, in part by how you related to me. There were times when you responded to me with such anger, blame, and shame. It was one of the most painful parts of the journey, because my own emotional wounds got all tangled up with yours. While a part of me knew it was a sign of a recent binge, another part of me questioned how I was contributing to your pain. I blamed myself. A lot of partners of addicts experience this and it is one of the most difficult aspects to this whole thing.

All of this has changed dramatically because of this process. I don't feel blamed for the shame you carried anymore. I feel more seen, heard, understood, and accepted. There's a lot more safety in our sex life now—there's transparency and trust. I know now more than ever that even when you disconnect from the truth and medicate, it isn't about me but about your pain. There's so much relief in knowing I can count on you to take responsibility for yourself because I have enough of my own work to do. Of course I still feel disappointed and hurt when you medicate, but I don't worry about it and I trust you. I know you are allowing your pain to be your teacher. I have witnessed your transformation and it gives me hope and courage to do the same. I'm so grateful I married you.

SETH: Of course this has made me a more loving and supportive husband. Where I used to locate my pain in my wife, I now locate it inside myself. This resulted in me ceasing (not overnight, but gradually) from trying to force her to change and focusing on changing myself. I stand as a loving witness to her transformation now, as she does for me. As I have learned to love myself, I have learned what it means to love her. I have also learned what it means to allow myself to be loved by her.

Our relationship had been built on a very unhealthy dynamic because we were two very wounded people trying to do intimacy. My pain mostly resulted in me having to take care of her and everyone else in the whole world, but not myself. This sucked me dry over time. But when healing started to come, I gained the ability to see the difference between loving someone and caretaking them. I set up boundaries. I started to be able to live my life; making choices with a clearer and clearer mind, and shedding the burdens I had carried for so long.

Typically when one member of an unhealthy dynamic decides to step into the light, both people start to see and feel things that have been under wraps for a long time. As my transformation took place, Amy started to feel left behind. Here I was, exploding into this new way of living life, ready and willing to tackle all the challenges I could, but my wife was still struggling to control her pain rather than work toward real transformation. And because marriage is a static link, to get to that life that I desired, it would be necessary either for her to join me on this path of transformation or for us to part ways.

We had some very honest talks about this and she started "the work" shortly thereafter. At the time of this writing, that was five years ago, and put succinctly: *everything has changed.* We live now with a very deep love for each other. Yes, we still fight, but these fights are few and far between and they don't last long. This has been a process of course, but after all this work over the last five years, there is a short "turnaround time" for us. We've healed so many of the things we once triggered in each other. It turns out we were each other's teachers.

We now have two children under the age of two, and they are our primary teachers. My little girl has been showing us both some very deep pain that we carry, and we are now working steadily to heal that pain. But there is work to be done so that we don't have to keep handing our burdens to our sweet daughter. My wife and I don't sleep much and are far too busy, and so that always brings about complications and barriers to intimacy, but there are *no* secrets between the two of us. Amy and I can talk about everything, including the deepest and darkest parts of our questions around sexuality.

A short note on the erotic, of which much more can be said: Yes, we talk about that too. Perhaps one of the greatest benefits to being free of shame is that you can finally communicate to your partner what you're thinking about and desiring/hoping for sexually. Without shame, we are able to gain the courage to be that vulnerable with our partners and ourselves. *And vulnerability is the core of intimacy.* If you walk this path, you could very well arrive at the same place we are, the place where *this* part of you becomes free, too. It's wonderful.

Has this changed the way you see your faith—what's that like?

If I were to sum up the largest change for me in this regard, it would be the absence of fear. When you lose all fear, faith changes a lot. Much of my confidence comes with the clarity and discernment one receives when shame is gone and one's spirit is alive; the question as to what I *do* is an entirely different one. As the Apostle Paul said, all things are permissible, but not all things are beneficial. Obviously, wisdom would dictate that I not do certain things. But as a result of this absence of fear, I can know the world and everything in it differently. I can love people outside of my circles authentically because they do not represent something I stand against in fear. I don't feel any need to judge people, only love them. I have to release fear and judgment in order to truly love.

But What About Jesus?

People inside the Christian church are always very interested in how this transformation has affected my beliefs regarding Jesus. Many people see the key issue to be my "atonement theory"—a theological way of addressing how God solves or has solved the problem of sin in the world through Jesus' death and resurrection on the Roman cross of crucifixion.

It would take another book for me to write about how my atonement theory has been impacted through this experience (and I would love to have that conversation should we run into each other somewhere, so feel free to ask), but for our purposes here, let me just say this: Jesus is central to this experience for me. I believe Jesus Christ is the center of the hourglass in this process of moving from one state of being to another. But I hold these beliefs and their intricate complexities with an open hand. I do not think one's beliefs regarding Jesus are the determining factor as to whether they can be transformed by the Spirit of God or not, though I do believe myself that Jesus is the Son of God. I believe the most important questions we can ask regarding Jesus is the same question He asked people: "What do you want?" I have experienced a God who meets us in our place of pain, our context, our spirits. And I think the life, death, and resurrection of Jesus Christ attest to God in this way.

In Moving Forward

There is no question I am still on this pilgrimage. The journey has become deeply sacred for me and I plan on continuing it for the rest of my life. I love my life and pray that you find the same peace with yours. Thank you for taking the time to read this book. May it bless you.

WELCOME TO THE PILGRIMAGE

The issue of porn addiction—both in and out of the Christian church—is a pressing one. The statistics on addiction are shocking, and spiritual leaders and pastors of either gender are in no way excluded from them. The presence of these addictions at the heart of our spiritual lives functions as a signal flare being sent out from the center of our religious systems, screaming out that there is something wrong with the way we understand our spirituality. If belief in a God who loves and rescues and redeems hasn't saved us from all our darkness, then what will?

In this book, we are pointing to a paradigm shift. This paradigm shift is meant not only for the way you understand sexuality, but for the way you *do* spirituality—your faith and understanding and experience of God. And this is for the believer and non-believer alike.

For far too long, we have been told that we are at war with the most sacred drives that exist inside of our bodies. Our minds have been held captive to control and belief while our spirits have been held underwater by some unseen force, powerless to do anything but push out one muffled scream after another in an attempt not to drown in a culture full of products, both religious and non-religious, that promise they will fill the hole in our core.

"One long muffled scream" is a great way to describe the state of my life after seven years of porn addiction and many more as a slave to depression and anxiety. When I had suffered enough, I laid down my sword, shed my armor, and began to seek another way—I call it "the third way."

That "third way" has become for me a "pilgrimage"—a Sacred Journey. I rechristened my struggles with addiction as a grace-filled, holy quest. I stopped wasting my energies on feeling guilty and ashamed of myself and instead started asking, "Why do I feel so guilty and ashamed?" It turns out I needed this addiction to show me the door to freedom, not just from the addiction itself, but also from all the things that seemed set on keeping me from ever knowing true happiness. The starting point was inside my body—deep within that horrible feeling of being frozen by fear, captive to worry and control; slave to my computer and the universe of medication that was available with the click of a button.

I felt it all *in my body,* so it seemed like a good place to begin—in my body. I was unable to move, desperately reaching up, hoping there was something real in the universe that could see my hand, grab it, and pull me out of the hole I had been living in. This was where I was, so this was where I began my pilgrimage.

I'm a Christian, so much of this journey has been spent on a quest for a deeper understanding of Jesus. This was one of my first realizations when I started this process: if I was going to follow the way of Jesus, then there had to be more depth to that experience than simply believing he was the son of God and *trying harder and harder* to do what he said. According to the Gospels, a very large portion of the ministry of Jesus of Nazareth was spent healing the broken—really healing them. He didn't lay hands on the sick and declare them "mostly free." Jesus seemed to do the opposite of that—he would meet people where they were, at their point of pain, removing shame and seemingly throwing it to the wind, and then often saying this interesting phrase: "Your faith has healed you."

Wait...

Did Jesus heal me or did I heal myself? Our perspective on this question seems to be incredibly important to our understanding of who God is and what it is to be spiritual beings designed by a loving Creator. Think about it for a second. We all feel this question in the deepest parts of us: Is there any real power? And if there is, then why don't we experience it more?

Why haven't *I* experienced it more?

We seem to be afraid of wrestling with these really huge questions because if we do, our identities might be stripped away, along with all the things we keep under such tight control. I don't know about you, but I don't want to fight a war anymore—I want to experience a peace that transcends understanding. I believe this struggle in our sexuality is the opposite of a battle. It is the sacred journey—the pilgrimage—to reconnect to the Spirit who gave birth to this Universe. And in that experience, I think we reconnect to ourselves. Jesus said the Kingdom of God is this mystery where all things are as they were designed to be. And he said this Kingdom is all around us all of the time, if only we have the eyes to see it. He said it's within us. Jesus was showing us a way home, back to God…back to ourselves. And this journey courses through every vein and lives in every heartbeat. It's something *you can feel inside.*

It feels like redemption.

So this is where we begin—all we who seek to be saved from whatever is inside of us that would drive us to self-hate and alienation, idolatry and darkness, or just plain unhappiness. This book is about something new. You might have no point of reference for my story, and you might find that unsettling or disorienting. That's okay, because that's how pilgrimage begins. You have to leave—you have to move. So lay down your sword, take a deep breath, and start walking...

Welcome to the pilgrimage.

chapter 1
LEARNING TO WALK

I'll begin where we all begin—where I grew up.

Growing up, there was a great deal of discussion in
my home regarding what it was to be saved. The word
"saved" was Christian-speak for "not going to hell when
you die," but you probably knew that already if you live
anywhere that has been touched by Evangelical Christian thinking. The people in my life spent tremendous
amounts of energy trying to determine who was saved
and who was not. The challenge was to try to figure out if
the person at the center of the discussion believed what
we understood to be the "true" doctrines that made you
a "true" Christian, which in our thinking was the only
way to be forgiven by God for your sins. As children, we
pretty much accept our experience as a source of truth,

so this question of who was and was not saved was tre-
mendously confusing.

I remember my first encounter with Mormons. I don't
think I had ever met such nice people before. I found it
difficult to believe my friend Joe in first grade was going
to hell, because he was the kindest person I had ever met,
even to this day. However, some of the really mean people
I knew at church were apparently saved, because they went
to our church and believed the right thing.

I was always told that God had made the rules and put
them in the Bible. My candy-obsessed kid-brain perceived
that no one could be as nice as Jesus, and if you didn't
believe in Jesus the way we did, you weren't forgiven for
your sins and therefore weren't "saved." No matter how
much peace and joy and happiness you had in this life,
you would pay for it big time later on. It seemed that being
saved required us to sacrifice this life and this earth and
most things that were fun for the sake of the afterlife where
we would be ushered through some pearly gates and go to
church for the rest of eternity.

I don't mean to critique those ideas here as much as to
simply state that this programming was my takeaway from
my childhood theological experience, and it was all very
confusing. If I sound angry about it... well, I am.

Sometimes I have conversations with friends that revolve
around that same inner programming. Like the one I had
recently with a friend of mine in Rwanda. We were taking a

break from work and he said to me in his accented English: "Hey, Seth, do you know this guy Enric who plays the music and lives in America now?" He was speaking about a mutual friend who had moved to the USA to go to school and pursue a music career.

"Yeah," I responded.

"He has the dreadlocks now," he said somewhat suspiciously.

"Yeah, he does."

"Some of these guys here," he said, "we think he is maybe not saved."

I smiled and shook my head, eyes cast to the ground.

Apparently, this musician who had decided to get dreadlocks was in danger of paying for the dreads by spending eternity in hell. I'm quite sure that when he was getting his dreadlocks, he wasn't thinking about this idea. He was more likely humming "Three Little Birds" by Bob Marley, and if you had asked him about the things he needed to be saved from in that moment, what would he have said?

When it comes to salvation, though, your average American needs to be saved from a few things more concerning than hair styles. Our divorce rate makes marriage look like a roll of the dice. The numbers regarding financial debt are staggering, along with crime, poverty, hunger, and addiction; not to mention boatloads of anxiety that manifest in corporate greed, abuse, and lives spent neglecting relationships in the hopes of making it. It is not a stretch to say that we need someone to throw us a lifeline. And the numbers are *no* different inside the Christian church than they are outside of it.

Books like this one exist because we feel the need to be *saved* so badly. While many Christians still adopt a perspective that to "be saved" is to end up in the right place after we die, to a growing number of people, it is no longer sufficient to point to a sacred text and claim that the text requires us to think more about the afterlife or pleasing a god than we do about the state of happiness or the lack thereof in our present lives. It is no longer acceptable to have to forsake hope for this life in "hopes" for the next. The gap between the pain we experience in the world and the things we claim to be "liberating truths" has grown too large. These beliefs that we are told are "true" are supposed to transform this world and this life here and now, *and I think that some part of us all knows it somewhere deep inside of us.*

For our purposes, we are going to mainly deal with pornography addiction, both outside and inside of the Christian church, where it has been described to me not as *a* crisis, but as *the* crisis of the modern era. A recent study indicates that 50% of men, including Christian pastors, use internet pornography on a regular basis, or could be described as "addicted." Strikingly, those who considered themselves fundamentalist Christians were 91% more likely to use porn than the median. For a group of people who claim to have a God-given truth that will set us free, there seems to be a significant gap between *believing* this truth and *experiencing* actual freedom. Or put another way: there is a huge difference between knowing this path and walking it — and that difference lies in our subconscious.

And this might be the most concise and authentic way to define addiction: unconscious suffering. Most of the suffering we experience is actually underneath what we experience on the surface.

There's a Latin phrase to describe this: *ordo salutis.* Translated, it means "order of salvation," an ordered system we create in the hopes of taming our beliefs and ourselves. This world has built one *ordo salutis* after another, whether it be religious belief systems that teach us to pacify a god created in a particular image, or economic and cultural systems that sell just another product, lifestyle, or dream to fulfill our unconscious suffering. The *ordo salutis* "saves" us from our pain.

However, the problem an *ordo salutis* presents is that *control* is not *healing.* Control, while giving us temporary relief from the symptoms of our pain, forces us to keep the pain with us, inside our bodies. Like a vault with too much contained inside, our pain will always find a way out. Our bodies begin to "leak" pain over time. Anxiety, depression, anger/rage, and addictions of all types are "leakages."

This overt expression of pain that exists at covert levels inside of us requires treatment, and so the *ordo salutis* takes hold and we begin to *medicate* the pain. Pick your drug; it can be anything. We all know people who medicate on "good" things (or more socially acceptable things) like religion and work, and we all probably know people who head the other way into some dark abyss of the "vices," if we haven't gone there ourselves. The effect is the same. We carry the pain with us still, masking the pain and controlling it instead of experiencing it and healing it. Therefore, when we are presented with one of these *orders of salvation,* obedience to these systems end up accomplishing something not that different than the addiction—we trade one prison for another and attempt to label our new prison as a place where we are "free."

I suppose that if you had lived your whole life in a tiny cell with no window and someone were to come along and punch a small hole in your wall where you could perhaps see a cloud or two against a sometimes blue backdrop, then that would probably feel a bit like freedom. But as I see it, these *orders of salvation* can actually be damaging, as they limit the upward potential of our spirits to heal us.

We are meant to live in the wild of what it is to be human, not in buildings and structures that never change or transform; adapting and learning in order to thrive, not just survive. So in this chapter, I will examine some of those structures of slavery/salvation and offer a critique that gave me a deeper way of understanding the problem of my porn addiction and set the stage to peel back the layers of what true freedom looked like for me and how I found it.

The Zombie Within

As a Christian kid growing up in Seattle in a Pentecostal (or "charismatic") church with less than healthy leadership dynamics, I had my fair share of religious-oriented pain. I not only had been taught I was inherently evil at the core, but also felt it at a visceral level. This left my stomach in knots when my 20s came calling. I attended a small Christian high school and a small Christian college and was married just before my senior year at the age of 27. I had never had any issues with habitual pornography to that point. Truth be told, I didn't even know what masturbation meant until I was 19. Guys in the locker room would make a joke about it and I would just laugh because I knew I was supposed to understand what that was.

When I got engaged my junior year in college, the difference in the level of intimacy triggered something deep and dark inside of me and I started feeling insecure. A new level of need, desire, and drive towards pornographic images rose up inside of me. But at the same time this darkness was awakened, so was the courage to overcome it.

I won't go into all the details of my attempts to learn Victoria's secret or the various ways I tried to fend off the shame and guilt of what I was doing in my nightly visits to the web. The details aren't always relevant to the real problem, so just know that I'm like you. I now don't believe my problem was a "sin" problem or an issue of "fleshly lust" as so many popular perspectives out there would claim. My problem was that I was asleep. Unconscious. If you had popped into my little apartment on one of those nights when I was doing my thing and had asked me why I was looking at those images and videos, I would have had an answer. I would have talked fast and spat out whatever I had been taught or come to accept for the sake of numbing myself to my pain.

I had beliefs (as I still do) which were a product of my life experiences. They were a natural human function of organizing those experiences into a system that was designed to protect me from whatever I needed protection from, whether from the outside or from within myself. I would probably be able to fend off most questions regarding why I was doing what I did. But, had I been asked the questions posed in this book, I would have had no choice but to say the words, "I don't know," and then the proverbial crap would have hit the fan, which in this case would have been a good thing. We all need our crap to hit the fan.

When my guilt and shame became a piano tied around my neck, dragging my life under, I finally looked into counseling. I told my wife, who at that point didn't know about my issues, that I needed some help with stress and went to a grad-student counselor the school provided for free to students. After several weeks I finally mentioned in passing

at the end of a session that I was having a little issue with
"lust." My counselor was a little shocked and unsure of what
to do, walking over to a bookshelf and handing me a copy of
the best-selling book *Every Man's Battle.*

"Maybe this will help you."

"Thanks," I said and walked out hopeful. Just looking at
the cover made me feel better. That was me, there on the
cover, walking down a peaceful beach alone, sun setting
gently in the pastel-soaked background. I was a good guy,
just like that guy, barefoot with jeans on. Where were my
shoes? I didn't know, but that was okay, because I was going
to win this battle. This was a real, visceral feeling I experienced as I looked at that cover. I wasn't alone anymore.

That was the real strength of the branding of that
book—it normalized the struggle for so many of us Christian dudes that were trying to do the right thing. It wasn't
just me; it was everybody. I knew that part to be true
because every friend I had was dealing with the same
issues, but I had never taken the time to feel that sense
of unity before. Something about that cover made me feel
not so alone. I still wish I could find the guy who made
that cover and give him a bear hug. I felt better walking
home with that book in my hands, even as the darkness
descended once again around me.

By the time I walked into my apartment, the knots in my
stomach had returned and my computer was glaring at me
from the corner of my tiny living space.

What Are You Medicating?

We are always making statements about who we think God is and what we think God is like, but within this quest for an authentic, spirit-driven freedom, it is necessary to give ourselves permission to doubt what we have believed or been taught—especially if those things aren't giving us life—and imagine a world where God might be different than we thought. The mere fact that we are addicted to *anything* should call into question some, if not all, of our beliefs. This is a crucial, yet challenging task.

I don't believe porn is the problem we are really dealing with. Making an enemy out of the pornography industry, though it is certainly a deeply dark and massive entity, will not free you from addiction. That industry exists for the same reasons you are struggling—a profound unconsciousness that allows darkness to move into the deepest parts of the human heart. We created the porn industry. It didn't create us. It continues to exist because we demand that it exist. But for now, you must understand we're not fighting a "battle." If we want war, we'll get it. If we seek peace, we will find it.

Porn isn't the problem; it's a medication *for* the problem. Like any pain pill, porn serves the purpose of keeping us from becoming conscious of the *real* problem. So, it will be very helpful from here on out to adopt this fundamental question: What are we medicating? If you can ask that question, you are already diving into a deeper level of consciousness.

chapter 2
THE ART OF
QUESTIONING

As I write this, my dog is curled up next to me sleeping. He's twitching a bit and keeps making sounds as
if he is dreaming. Perhaps he is dreaming of saving my
life or something. More likely, he's dreaming of anything
resembling meat. What I know for sure is that he is most
definitely unconscious. Part of his body is hanging off of
the couch like a limp noodle.

We will use the word "conscious" in all its forms a great
deal in this book, and I know to some it can sound "new-
agey," but just know that consciousness is best understood
as what we see and what we don't see. If you are asleep
like my dog, for instance, you are not terribly aware of what
is going on around you. You are unconscious. If you are

dreaming, you are a little more conscious. If you wake up, you are more conscious still.

But then we begin to deal with the distance between our waking conscious thoughts and our subconscious motivations. We carry baggage, pain, and all kinds of complex things in our subconscious until they find their way out through our decisions and behaviors. This is why we can *think* we are a certain type of person who has a certain way of being in the world while at the very same time, the people around us experience something radically different. Every person lives at different levels of consciousness, and everyone forms beliefs and thoughts that spawn action *from that level of consciousness.* We also interpret teaching and text from those levels. The Bible especially can be—and often is—used as a weapon of judgment and condemnation when read from a certain level of consciousness. When there is no ability to see below the surface into the deeper chambers of human spiritual existence because of blinding shame and guilt, then it becomes easy to see human nature as something that must be caged and tamed through an *ordo salutis,* or "order of salvation" that can prove the "disciplining power of the faith."

The Hand We Were Dealt

The shame/behavioral paradigm commonly ignores the hurtful origins of our pain and thus the addictions which medicate that pain. These origins become buried deep in our stories and we give little credence to them, virtually guaranteeing the pain stays exactly where it is. It is certainly easier to control our guilt and shame by labeling our behaviors as sin than it is to turn and face the pain we're medicating. Who *wants* to feel their pain? We know it is there, but as the Irish philosopher Peter Rollins says, "we don't want to *know* that we know."

Patrick Carnes, in his book *Don't Call It Love*, writes, "A temptation exists to view childhood events as ancient history. Early in therapy, families often question the use of 'dredging up the past' or rousing the 'sleeping dogs' that have been put to rest. The myth is that those events are over." Though these events are the source of our suppressed pain, Carnes does point out that no one else can be held responsible for the addicts' behavior. This is often the point where many religious people plant their feet and cease their exploring, deeply afraid of the idea that an issue is *anyone's* fault but the addict's. As a way of shielding us from truly confronting the pain that exists in our subconscious, an *ordo salutis* is built to support the myth that we can be perfect, that we can simply follow a teaching and achieve perfection, no matter what we carry inside of us.

While I would like to offer a new way of approaching this problem and even practical steps towards freedom based on a deeper examination of what it means to be humans created in the image of the Divine, I will not presume to speak *for* the Divine and thus create just another *ordo salutis.*

Instead, I will attempt to dive deeper into the human experience of the Divine and determine what that experience says about who we are and how we heal.

One Problem - How Do We Know What is True?

Good question. And this seems to be the big hang-up in so much of the thinking we find in our culture, especially in the church: it seems we are often expected to gauge the truth of what we're taught based on whether it matches a system of orthodoxy, or "right belief;" it matters not whether it works or has any actual effect. The word "faith" is usually employed in this way: believe something blindly, and ask no evidence as to the truth of it besides matching up with doctrinal systems of belief. Discount your experience and your desire and adhere to a system of belief, a standard of purity written by that belief, and a structure of discipline contained within that belief that holds consequences for you of epic proportions should you fail. You also have to discount any stories you hear about someone gaining freedom outside of the religious or scientific boundaries you adhere to. That is a difficult place to be — it is driven by a deep fear of the unknown and by a god, both religious and scientific, who seems to be afraid of that unknown as well.

Often in our world, there is more concern with maintaining the *belief systems,* both religious and non-religious, than with finding *freedom* at all costs. But I contend that we are free to gauge whether something is *true* or not based on our experience of it.

"Faith" is the courage to hear and act upon the stories that speak to the truth: stories that manifest the presence of God (also called "the kingdom of God") in this world, which usually looks like peace, hope, love, mercy, kindness, and patience. If we follow a path that shows this evidence and then experience the same freedom we witness in those stories, then we should move towards that source, trusting that our spirits—that part of us that is connected to the Spirit of God—can and will lead us to the truth.

The Prison of Lists

Lists are very prominent in the shame/behavior sobriety models, lists of dos and don'ts for your mind and body, lists of requirements, lists of rights and wrongs. Not only do these lists paint a picture of a prison with slightly larger windows than the one currently occupied, they also crowd one's mind with scapegoats. If I can place *any* responsibility for what I am doing on that woman jogging on the sidewalk on a beautiful summer day, rather than deal with my problem, my vision becomes clouded by judgment of the jogger and I am that much less able to approach the real source of the problem: the pain that lies in my subconscious. It also turns that fictional jogger into a source of medication rather than a person who is an object of Divine love. And the inevitable perspective I will adopt towards those who fall into my list, such as those making those movies or the jogger is that they are part of the problem and must therefore be evil as well.

Again, the intent of these perspectives is to help you find some distance between you and the addiction that has been crushing your ability to live free. That's a good thing! But lists leave out the notion that there is a freedom deeper than simply avoiding the medication. And if we don't believe that, then we must at least acknowledge the possibility that we aren't actually talking about God anymore.

Deus Ex Machina

In his book *Insurrection,* Peter Rollins exposes this behaviorally motivated way of thinking as a system meant to protect us from the unconscious pain we carry rather than address the true nature of the problem. In expanding on some of the later ideas of Dietrich Bonhoeffer, who had become concerned that "the Christian understanding of God had been largely reduced to the status of a psychological crutch," Rollins describes how we invent an image of God that we need in order to fulfill a task rather than to express a lived reality.

Bonhoeffer used the term *deus ex machina* ("god out of the machine") to describe this phenomenon. The term comes from ancient Greek theatre, originally referring to a climactic moment when a behind-the-scenes machine would lower a supernatural being onto the stage to alter the action. The word evolved to mean something entirely different when lazy playwrights started introducing divine characters on a whim for the purposes of buttoning up a story without having to truly do the work of resolving plot lines. Rollins believes that the god we are actually invoking through all our lists and behavioral prescriptions, is a form of *deus ex machina*—a god made in the image we choose for it, meant to resolve our doubts and suppress our pain. This type of god is seemingly capable of holding grace in one hand and shame in the other, and we feel it all at the deepest of levels.

This shame-driven interpretation of the character of God serves the same purpose I mentioned earlier: it allows us to maintain residence in our prison and control our pain without fully confronting or experiencing it. In this prison, God is the warden; if we can show good behavior, or achieve purity (or what we think of as "purity"), then we might possibly move into a better cell. Perhaps parole even awaits us, where we can walk the streets and claim a certain type of "freedom." But true freedom, the kind Christ speaks of when truth is lived out, is out of reach. And we are told that we should be okay with this by so many of the people that claim to speak the truth about God.

Deconstruct Me

In moving forward, we must do the hard but good work that so many do not, whether by choice or because they simply aren't aware of any other way: we must go backwards. This is the narrow path. We must do subtraction inside of ourselves rather than addition, removing barriers to what already exists within our deepest parts rather than adding one more tool, one more word, or one more belief on top of what has become a cluttered and chaotic soul. We must deconstruct the systems in our life where we store our pain, systems such as the culture we create, the language we use, and the beliefs we possess. We must take them apart piece by piece and see what they reveal.

Michelangelo said his statue of David was waiting inside the stone for its time to be revealed. Such is the Divine nature inside of us all, if only we are willing to do the work of chipping away the stone. This Divine nature is addicted to nothing, knows true happiness, and possesses untold power to transform not only us, but also the world around us. So, let us begin this deconstruction with something simple that we've already begun to approach: words.

Chapter 3
WORDS AND MEANING

There is a series of videos on the internet that have in some way or another the title "Sh-t (subculture) says," which feature some of the stereotypical terms or phrases you might hear from that subculture. One such video is dedicated specifically to evangelical Christians and is titled "Shoot Christians Say." The video is a well-edited blitzkrieg of a language that has come to be known as "Christianese." Two Christian dudes, in this case two twenty-something, white, American, evangelical Christian dudes, converse with one another in a casual tone of comical assumption that people understand them. Phrases like "It's a God thing," "Guard her heart," and "We're gonna get some dudes tonight and *fellowship*" mix with about a zillion names for small church groups and Christian conferences (*Ignite* being my favorite). The video was brilliantly made, both cleverly funny and strangely numbing in the same instance—a tribute to the power and importance of semantics in the human experience.

"Christianese" isn't unique in the world. Every culture and subculture has its language—a set of assumed meanings. The first time I was in London and someone asked me for a "fag," I was taken aback. After a brief second, he realized I wasn't from around there and redirected his vernacular: "a cigarette, mate."

You can probably think of a time when you made a similar mistake. This is what Shakespeare was getting at when he had Hamlet reply to a question about what he was reading with a simple, "words, words, words." To use an analogy, words are a backpack, ready to travel. Meaning is the baggage stuffed into the pack through a lifetime of learning, living, and suffering. As we carry these burdens in our lives, we begin to attach words to our experiences, eventually solidify like drying cement. They harden into belief systems that can isolate us from a world of people who see the world differently than we do. So, in order for us to know each other and, more importantly, to know ourselves, we must empty the backpacks, one piece at a time.

As an example, I have a friend who is married with three children. He has begun to explore some deep pain in his life and why it leads to certain negative behaviors; as he has done this, his life experiences have required new ideas and new language to frame it. The old words could still work, but for him and everyone else around him, the old words still seem attached to old beliefs and old ways of thinking that left him oppressed and struggling. What is changing for him is his religious thinking.

At the same time, his wife still ascribes to those beliefs that he now finds painful to hold. She still values the old words and the old beliefs and claims that the spiritual bond she desires in her marriage can only exist if she and her husband believe the same things. To keep the peace, he could use the old words while still meaning something completely different than she does. Of course, this could become a strange type of prison very quickly where my friend would be forced to live in silence, mimicking an existence that isn't true or meaningful to him. He faces a choice — introduce new words and rock the boat or continue to walk lifeless through his world, hoping to avoid the appearance of conflict.

In an effort to discover the true freedom from "sin" that each of us at some level wants to believe is possible, we must engage in a type of deconstruction — a way of disassembling the parts of a thing so we can see what it's made of. If we take the struggles we have with addiction and begin to take them apart piece by piece, starting with the words we speak, we will start to discover that we are a created being that is designed in our core to be completely connected to ourselves, the ones we love, and our Creator, unafraid and free from shame.

The Language of Biff

To illustrate how this language plays a part in the fasci-
natingly complex world of pornography addiction in the
Christian church (as an archetype for all addiction), I will
use the example of a young college student, a dear friend
of mine whom I'll call Biff (yes, in reference to *Death of
a Salesman*). He played on a soccer team that a friend of
mine coached and had been praying God would give him a
mentor when I came along and fit the bill.

At our first meeting, I started by telling him a little bit
about myself and then asked him why he wanted this relationship and what he hoped to receive from this experience.

"You mean you want to hear my testimony?" he said.

I smiled at the word "testimony." This kid had been
raised old-school, like me. Biff wasn't aware that I spoke
his language, but it was helpful, because he was so well-
versed in the language and moved at such a pace that
there was very little room for clarification. His Christianese
was perfect, flawless in its ability to convey nothing while
conveying everything a fellow believer like myself would
need to hear in order to have a conversation that meant
something and nothing at the same time, affirming my own
beliefs while not challenging any of them.

At one point, as he was telling about the way his parents
divorced but still loved each other, his tone went quiet and
his eyes diverted downward slightly from their ever-present
up-and-to-the-left position.

"And I've had a struggle, you know, with lust."

There it was—the word *lust*; a wonderful term with a long etymological history, but best known as being one of the members of the exclusive "Seven Deadly Sins." It was almost like one of those speed bumps you stopped taking seriously a long time ago and now just rumble over with your car, knowing your shocks can handle it. He cruised on at a dizzying pace. It was clear that this was a young man with a great deal of pain to protect, so intricate was the labyrinth of his words. But I saw myself in him, a few years ago, unconsciously clinging to each word like a buoy keeping me afloat. Biff simply wasn't aware of these things at any conscious level. I knew all too well the type of prison he was living in.

As he rumbled on, I interrupted him.

"How long have you been a porn addict?"

He stopped short and I could see he was holding his breath.

"Well, I don't know if it's an addiction," he said quietly.

"Can you stop?" I asked.

His answer was somewhat erratic. It sounded a bit like this: "Well, I am not sure....if I really wanted to...maybe. Probably. I'm not sure."

The word *addiction* is a tough one. It triggers a sense of powerlessness inside of us. It says we *can't* stop. It assigns meaninglessness to our faith, whether it is a faith in God or in a sense of personal power and self-control. It is also a word that conjures up some horrifying images of the destruction we see all around us caused by addiction every-day. Jesus said, "You will know the truth and the truth will set you free." But if we don't feel free, then we can simply change the definition of the word *free* at multiple levels inside of us. This knowledge keeps us from needing to explore the unresolvable in our lives and in the world. Like some friends of mine have told me: "Let's focus on what we can know, not on what we can't know."

The problem remains though, just like the Apollo Astronauts: we live in a situation where the only thing protecting us from the vast vacuum of space is a fabric no thicker than a piece of tinfoil. That "unknown" on the other side of the tinfoil is where all the pain resides, and we must go there in order to know true freedom.

The Man Who Knew Too Little

The Bill Murray comedy, *The Man Who Knew Too Little* is a fun example of this. In this story, Wallace Richie (Murray) is an employee of Blockbuster Video in Des Moines, Iowa ("he's in the movie business") and is heading to London to visit his big-shot banker brother. While there, he attends the latest craze in live theatre, the "Theatre of Life." It's an interactive experience where the participant plays a sponta-neous role as the hero in an action-packed crime thriller. At the very same time that Murray's character is beginning the fantasy, there is a real espionage scenario, of which he is

not aware, playing out all around him. Some seedy characters are trying to bring back the Cold War by organizing a
terrorist attack and pinning it on the Russian government.

Simply by chance, the two scenarios stumble across
each other and Murray's character ends up accidentally
playing the role of a real spy in a real spy scenario, all the
while thinking he's an actor in a play, posing as a spy. As
expected, the madness ensues and we all laugh because
we are in on the joke. The unconsciousness of reality is the
core of comedy. Or put another way: we wouldn't laugh if
Wallace Richie were to awake to the situation around him.
We'd be afraid for him.

Let's take a closer look at the reasons why Wallace Richie
never seems to become conscious of his predicament.
There is a shared vocabulary and shared assumptions linked
to the vocabulary being employed by the actors in The Theatre of Life and the real spies. In one of my favorite scenes,
the bad guys, thinking Richie is an assassin working with
them, are using a code language to ask about whether
Richie (code name: Spencer) has disposed of his apparent
target, a girl name Laurie:

Bad Guy #1 to Bad Guy #2: "Ask him if he has elimi-
nated the girl?"

Bad Guy #2 to Spencer: "Spencer. Did you take the girl
to the bathroom?"

Spencer (Richie) of course didn't kill the girl and the girl
has happened to go to the bathroom to "freshen up." And

seeing that Richie isn't conscious of the real-life scenario playing out around him, he simply answers honestly,
although unconsciously.

Spencer to Bad Guy #2: "No. She went to the loo,
by herself."

Bad Guy #2 to Bad Guy #1, after contemplative pause:
"By herself? Suicide."

Bad Guy #1 to Bad Guy #2: "Finally a spot of luck. Ask
him if he's disposed of the body."

Bad Guy #2 to Spencer: "Spencer. Did you flush?"

Spencer to Bad Guy #2: "Well, I think she's going to do
that, don't you Pal? I'll ask her. Laurie!?"

Bad Guy #2 to Bad Guy #1: "He's talking to her!"

Bad Guy #1 to Bad Guy #2: "She's still in the bowl?"

Bad Guy #2 to Bad Guy #1: "Maybe he tried to flush her
but she floated back up!"

Bad Guy #1 to Bad Guy #2: "Tell him to flush her! Spencer knows how to deal with floaters! Tell him to use the
plunger or we're sunk!"

The scene illustrates the function of language in the
most simple yet illuminating of ways. Wallace Richie's
illusion was made a reality through the use of language
he had been trained to accept as reality. There are even
some points in the film where Bill Murray's character starts
using the dialect of an actor ("May I break character for a
second?") instead of a spy, which creates a jarring effect
that would have broken the illusion had the Bad Guy

characters not been so comically dense. Thus, Richie is allowed to stay in this reality, and this is what makes the comedy work. The point is made though—the language is both the element that has put him in danger while simultaneously protecting him from the knowledge of that danger.

More than once in the film, a bad-guy assassin has a gun pointed at Wallace Richie. If at any point, the bad-guy had pulled the trigger, the first thing to die would not have been Richie himself, but his illusion that he was or ever had been okay.

Some people have referred to this type of human experience as a "faith crisis" while others have called it "dying to self." It is a loss of identity and it is fundamentally just what it sounds like—a death. It is painful and earth-shattering and messy beyond belief. And, it's not at all funny, which is probably why (spoiler alert!) Bill Murray's movie did not include this scenario.

One thing we know for sure about this death is that it is inevitable. If it doesn't take place here in this life, some form of it will most likely occur as we approach death. We may not know what happens after we die, though there is no shortage of ideas, but we know that everyone dies eventually, and coming to grips with this reality tends to strip people of all need to pretend anymore. All identities fall away. If we choose to avoid this death to our identity at all costs in this life, we will take our unconsciousness to the grave... but we're still going to the grave.

In the film, even after Wallace Richie has success-
fully if unknowingly thwarted the terrorist plot, the final
scene has him and the girl sitting on a beach where they
are approached to work as an assassin for "The Team."
Richie, of course, assumes "The Team" is a well-known
theatre company, though we the viewers are aware it's a
secret agency that deals in assassination. He accepts and
we are left with an inevitable sense of "how long can he
keep this up?"

We all know *someone* who is barely hanging on to whatever they *think,* whether consciously or unconsciously, is
going to fulfill them, while *knowing* at some level that it
won't. Or maybe we're the one in that situation. We're all
asking the question, "How long can they keep this up?"

So, to return to my friend Biff: the word *lust*, not unlike
the word *sin*, is burdened by particular theologies that
stress the total depravity of human beings and a conserva-
tive view of "original sin." It has functioned as an agent
that has both put him in danger and also protected him
from the knowledge of that danger. It has endangered him
by pushing him into a cycle of sin and repentance that
seems to have no end because it has driven his sexuality
into the unconscious world, and it has protected him from
danger because it has held the necessary and inevitable
death of all the illusions at bay. This protection is only
temporary and must come to an end in order for the light
to be shed on the unconscious pain and in order to find

freedom. What that end looks like can vary from a graceful disillusionment—something that gently frees you—to
a sometimes violent event—tragedy that shocks so greatly
you have no reference for what just happened.

Simply put, it's going to hurt, no matter what. This is why
most people in the realm of addiction and its treatment are
familiar with the term "rock bottom." It is the place where
most people have to go in order to find actual freedom.

Did you catch that? Most people *choose* suffering in order
to *avoid* suffering.

The difference is in the consciousness. Most of us would
much rather suffer unconsciously and medicate that pain
than suffer consciously and find freedom. The pain we are
medicating didn't necessarily begin through our decisions,
but we continue in it through a mixture of unconscious
and conscious choices. If we can't accept responsibility for
those choices, then we are at an impasse.

And it is an entirely different matter to pursue freedom.

chapter 4
FEELING EVERYTHING

So what changed for me? It all started with my twin brother Dave. And since his story is unique to him, I'll let him tell it.

DAVE: In light of what we know is out there, it almost sounds cliché now: I had been dealing with a porn addiction for over 10 years. It was never an "addiction" until after I was married and especially once I had internet in the house, around year three. But the truth is, like most people dealing with porn, I had been hunting for sensual images since I was very little.

Like many of us, I read every book and sought help from every source I had available to me inside the church and my Christian circles. And for a while, those things helped and I found myself "sober." I understood that sobriety was the standard for freedom but when I arrived there, but I also found that I didn't *feel* any happier. The guilt had certainly lessened but the long-promised freedom never seemed to materialize internally.

Important note: I have always considered freedom something you would feel. You could call it "inner peace" or an overall feeling of victory over that which enslaves you. Either way, it was something to be felt, rather than just a cognitive understanding that you were, in fact, free. There's been a popular offensive waged against the concept of "feeling" in popular American Christian thought, teaching us to not trust what we feel but rely on what we "know," namely how we interpret what the Bible teaches us about everything.

But I find that way of thinking unhelpful. For those who believe in a Creator, we must also believe that God made emotions, the nervous system, hormones... the whole "feelings package." It seems that there is a mandate to feel, given to us by our Creator.

I wanted to feel totally free, as in "walk past the Victoria's Secret in the mall without anxiety" kind of freedom. As in "SI Swimsuit pop up ad, easily click-and-close, keep on being productive" kind of freedom. But the general message out there was that it wasn't possible.

When things got hard, I went back to porn. I went back to hiding it from my wife. I pulled away from the men's groups and the therapy books that no longer seemed to help me. Eventually, I hit rock bottom and I decided to end my life. And for whatever reason, I admitted this to my wife. It didn't go over well.

A Fortuitous Phone Call

A few days later I got a phone call from my brother-in-
law Andrew, who had been working with a non-traditional
counselor named Floyd for the past few years, trying out an
alternative form of therapy. Growing up in my church, I had
been more-or-less taught that if you opened the door to the
Devil, he and all his legions would jump right in and have
a hay-day inside you. But I had hit rock bottom and the
conversation ended up going something like:

Andrew: "Why don't you just go talk to Floyd. It
couldn't hurt."

Me: "Dude, I don't want to go do a bunch of chanting.
I'm just... it's not what I want to do. I'm gonna get some
counseling at church."

Andrew: "You don't have to do any chanting, man. You
can just go and talk to him."

Me: "I can just talk?"

Andrew: "Yes."

Me: "... okay."

This was me saying, "If Satan had a solution, I'm ready to
listen." I simply had nothing to lose.

It was December 2, 2009. The counseling center was
actually just a large, split-level house in a nice, middle-
class neighborhood in Anchorage, Alaska where I live. A
married couple named Marianne and Floyd ran it, both of
them as practitioners, with Marianne handling the day-
to-day business. When I got there, I took off my shoes (a

common practice in Alaskan homes) and took a seat on the living room couch. Floyd is a Southeast Alaska Native, with a gray ponytail, glasses, and a well-groomed mustache. He greeted me and handed me a clipboard.

"It's a questionnaire," he said. "There are no wrong answers but make sure you answer every question." The questions were therapy-ish. "Have you ever been diagnosed with depression?" "Do you have any addictions?" I quickly wrote down that I had been a porn addict for over 10 years.

Marianne and Floyd sat across from me in separate chairs. I scanned the room for artifacts, finding a small jade Buddha, several feathers, lots of pagan-looking stuff, a large library of books of all sorts, and a great deal of Southeast Alaskan artwork: beadwork, paintings, and carvings.

Floyd was perusing my paperwork. "You've never had any tragedy in your life?" he asked.

"Well... I lost my father when I was twelve," I replied. "I forgot to write that down."

He handed me the clipboard. "You should write that down," he said.

I had somehow missed that question. I quickly wrote down that my father had been killed in a plane crash when I was twelve years old. He was a missionary, flying an airplane out of Nairobi, Kenya for a division of an American missions organization. His plane had gone down in Southern Sudan, and it was suspected that it had been shot down. However it happened, my brother and two sisters and

I had grown up without our father.

And Floyd and Marianne seemed to find this significant.

What Do You Want?

"What do you want to get out of today's session?"

Floyd and Marianne had taken some time to explain their style of therapy to me. They talked about "moving energy" that was trapped in our bodies, that our natural state of being was one of peace and oneness with God, and that pain and suffering blocked that connection. In their view, healing was possible and involved removing those blocks. I still didn't know what that meant, but the question on the table made sense to me.

"What do you want to get out of today's session?"

At that point, I had never articulated the idea to myself but the words came out of my mouth instantly.

"You know what I really want? I have this knot... in my chest. It really hurts and I think it's been there a long time. I'd really like to know what it is. Can you tell me?"

"Would you like to know?" he asked.

"Yes, very much."

"Okay, you're ready. Let's go do some work."

Marianne smiled with excitement while Floyd got up from his chair. I became very nervous and tried to make some excuses about how I didn't have a ton of time and could come back another day but Floyd gently led me up a few stairs and through a heavy curtain into an open room with a cream-colored carpet. There were more new-age artifacts: crystals, feathers, Alaska Native masks and artwork, native drums, and, in the center of the floor, a cushioned pad and pillow.

"Lay down here, on your back," Floyd motioned. After I did so, he covered me with a blanket up to my shoulders. "Put your arms at your side," he said. He then covered my eyes with a sleep mask.

"What's the blindfold for?" I asked.

"It will help you concentrate better, keep you from distractions," he replied.

From the point that Floyd had said, "You're ready," my mind had been racing, desperately trying to find a way out of the session. But here I was, blindfolded, on my back, covered up. And I couldn't escape. So I gave in. *If the devil is going to get me, then so be it. I give up*, I thought, and tuned in to Floyd's voice. He knelt by my left side.

"Now breathe," he said. "Take deep breaths. Fill your whole body with air, all the way down to your toes."

I began to try and fill up my lungs, much more than normal. As I did this, Floyd began to speak words that now have become sacred to me:

"Young man... all your life, you've been taught not to feel. All of us men have been taught not to feel. You've been told to 'Tough it up!' 'No tears!' 'Be tough!' No more... Today, we're going to feel everything. Are you ready?"

I nodded.

"Now I want you to breathe faster, like you're running uphill," he said.

After six or seven fast, deep breaths, it began. I felt a stutter in my breathing and began to subtly choke on the air. Floyd kept coaching me to keep breathing; I tried but the choking got worse.

"What... is... happ...ening..." I said.

Floyd kept saying softly, "Stay in it. Keep breathing."

As I write this, it's been years since that day, but I can still feel that moment. It was the moment the entire world turned upside down for me and everything changed. It is the moment my spirit came alive.

Amidst the breathing and stuttering, it was as if a crack appeared in my shell and someone ripped it wide open. My body arched up into the air and I screamed. It felt as if I was feeling every emotion I had ever stuffed down inside myself since the day I was born. Intense grief and sadness, violent anger and rage... even laughter. It was all coming out of me and it was painful as anything I had ever felt.

After a minute of screaming, my body settled back to the floor and I began sobbing heavily. Floyd sat next to me, softly encouraging me to stay in it, to let it out, to keep breathing. At this point I knew something important was happening to me and that I should allow it to continue so I gave myself up to it and listened closely to Floyd's words.

After several minutes of this, the grieving seemed to slow. Floyd then asked me if I could see anything in my mind.

"Focus in your mind. Where are you?" he asked.

As I obeyed, I could see clearly that I was in the living room at our home in Nairobi. Looking around, I could tell this was the day I had learned of my father's death.

That day my brother and I had been at a friend's house, playing wiffleball. I had hit a home run, knocking the ball on their roof, which was a rare feat so I was on cloud nine. A friend of my father's had come to the house to drive us home, and when I asked if I could sit in the front seat, he said "Of course." When we arrived, I found several of my parents' friends sitting on our couches, one of them comforting my sobbing mother.

My 9-year-old sister Ruth looked at me blankly and then came up and whispered, "Dad's dead."

It was this scene to which I had returned in the vision. I told Floyd where I was. He then asked, "Who's there?"

"Friends of my parents. My sisters," I replied. "Ruth is just looking at me."

"She's in shock," said Floyd.

"Everyone is looking at me."

"They're all in shock," he said.

All of a sudden, I could see an opaque wall growing like liquid in front of me, rising between me and everyone else in the room. I described this to Floyd.

"You're protecting yourself."

Instantly, the vision shifted and I was in the same room but my father was there, sitting at the dinner table. The mourners were gone. I described the scene to Floyd. "This is the last time I saw my father," I said.

"What is he doing?" he asked.

"He's getting up to leave." He was heading out the door, bound for Sudan.

"Tell him not to go," said Floyd. In my mind, I directed the young me to stand in front of him. I said aloud, "Dad, don't go." But in the vision my father simply walked around me, not even acknowledging my presence. Floyd urged me to use force, to block the door. I did this and my father grabbed me by the shirt, slamming me against the wall and walking out the door in a huff.

In that moment, I screamed, "No! *NO!* Don't go! *You're going to die!*" And then the strangest thing came out of my mouth: "This isn't f'n Viet Nam!!!"

There was a moment of silence. Then Floyd said, "Yes, it is."

"What?"

"Your father is still in Viet Nam. He has to go. He lived and his friends died and he is stuck in that place. He has to go. He has a death wish," explained Floyd.

In that moment, a truth flooded in like a wash of warm water over my brain. For my whole life, my father had been held up as a hero and a martyr. Never had it crossed my mind, not even for an instant, that he had had a choice whether to fly there or not. That he had four children and a wife back in Nairobi was of little significance when a man was bringing the Word of God to someone. While that seems a noble goal, I now realized he had made a selfish choice. He had not valued his life high enough and had been led, unconsciously, into a place where he should not have been. His choice had in turn doomed his family to a life without him and all that that would entail.

Even as I write this now, I realize how judgmental I might sound. Part of my truth in that moment was the understanding that I had the right to grow up with a father. This was "my truth." His hero status disappeared before my eyes and he became a normal man, suffering like the rest of us, trying to find adventure, running from problems, happy to be flying in a danger zone rather than safe at home with his family. And the truth of this broke my heart. I lay there on the floor and sobbed, crushed by this new understanding.

Floyd reached down, helped me up off the floor, removed the blindfold, and said, "Let me tell you about what your father missed."

Gently holding me by the arm, he walked me in a slow circle around the room. "Your father never saw you grow. He never saw you become the great athlete you are. He would have loved seeing you play. He never saw you graduate from high school. He would have been so proud of you..." With each word, it felt as though I was being stabbed in the heart. I sobbed and sobbed, agreeing aloud with each thing, saying, "No... he never saw me play basketball..."

Floyd continued, "He never met Maria. He wasn't there to see you married. She looked so beautiful. He never met his grandchildren..." This broke my heart and I cried out, "They're so beautiful! You missed it! You would've loved them!" And Floyd continued, citing my growth as a man and everything he knew of me until I became overwhelmed and collapsed on my knees. I cried and cried until there were no tears left.

I spent two hours with Floyd that day and we never discussed religious beliefs. It wasn't a concern at that point. In even making that appointment, I was admitting that my beliefs had failed me because, after all, aren't our beliefs supposed to be the anchors that ground us and give us a place to stand? But there, in those two hours, belief was suspended and the only thing that mattered was the experience of the moment. And it was healing me.

When the tears finally subsided, I rested on my knees, utterly exhausted, while Floyd slipped the blindfold back over my eyes and knelt in front of me. He held my hands in his.

"David, I want you to call your father back to you now," he said. Lifting my head, I softly called to my father to appear before me and he did. I remember subtly wondering about how easy it was. I was blindfolded and yet a vision of my father was clear as day before me. He wore the same yellow ball cap and jean jacket. It was the image of my father I most related to.

"Is he here?" asked Floyd.

"Yes," I replied.

"Good... now tell him... it's time to go."

As I tried to look into my father's eyes, he resisted, looking down. "He won't look at me," I said to Floyd.

"Tell him to look at you," he said.

"Dad... look at me." He continued to look at the floor. "He won't look at me. He keeps looking down."

"He's ashamed," said Floyd. "You don't ask... you *tell* him to look at you. Take his face." And at this, Floyd took my hands and placed them on his own face. Concurrently, in the vision I took my father by the face and said, "*Look* at me." It reminded me of when I would scold one of my sons. Finally, he reluctantly locked my eyes in his.

"I have him," I said to Floyd.

"There's a light opening up behind him. Do you see it?" Floyd asked.

"Yes," I said as a door of light opened behind my father.

"Tell him to go into the light," said Floyd.

"Dad, you have to go. It's time. Time to go," I said. And my father began to step back slowly.

As he did this, Floyd slowly pulled his hands out of my own.

"Tell him to go," Floyd continued to encourage me.

"Go, Dad." And finally, I could see he was relieved. He stepped into the door and, as Floyd pulled his hands out of mine, the door closed. It went completely dark.

That moment was the strangest for me. My body went instantly cold. I began shivering as if I had stepped outside without my coat (keeping in mind, it was hovering around zero degrees outside, typical of a December day in Anchorage, Alaska). "What's happening? I'm freezing... it's so dark..." The truth of that moment was that I was terrified. I don't remember ever feeling so isolated and alone before.

"Your father has been with you for a long time. You've let that go and now you're alone," explained Floyd. "But look into the dark... really look."

I did and saw nothing.

"Look... what do you see?" Floyd asked. And as I focused on the dark, a twelve-year-old boy walked towards me. "It's me," I said.

"Good," said Floyd. "Why don't you try giving him a hug?"

So I did. And as I did this, the twelve-year-old boy melted into my body.

How do I describe that moment? It felt like a soul-massage, with a warm feeling that washed over my body and so relaxed me that I hit the floor. I let out an audible "aaahhh-hhhhh...." and rested there. I felt a peace inside my body I had never felt before. It was lovely. I moved my hand slowly around my chest, amazed at how clean it all felt. I lay there, crying softly, but these were tears of gratitude. I could feel gratitude coursing through me like electricity.

We exited the room where Marianne was waiting with a big hug. "You were really moving some energy up there! Awesome!" she said.

I was in a bit of a daze and said "Thank you."

Going down the stairs, I began putting on my shoes. I

looked up at Floyd, standing on the top of the stairs, smiling. "What do I do with this?" I asked. "I don't know what to do."

"Don't worry," Floyd said, calmly. "When it's time, you'll know what to do. But for now, don't talk about it. People won't understand. And come back. You have much more work to do."

And with that, I walked out the door.

chapter 5
WHAT WE BELIEVE

SETH: While reading Dave's story, what did you experience? Were you struggling to believe him? Did you feel judgmental? Compassionate? Hopeful? Fearful? What is the difference between all of these things?

Whatever you experienced while reading it, understand that Dave's story has an implication for your story. Dave's story is a type of trailhead: a story of an experience of freedom that marks the possibility of a new path. You might not know what the path looks like for you, and neither do I, but you now know there is a path there. And if you're up for something new, then let us dive into something Dave began to speak of in his story regarding belief and what power, if any, it possesses.

In order to defeat addiction, whether we are religious or not, we are required to engage our belief systems in an entirely different way from what we're used to, like stepping outside of them to observe them. Think of it as putting all of your beliefs in an aquarium, turning on the tank lights, turning off the room lights, and then just gazing at the tank for no reason other than observation.

There are consequences when we begin to observe our beliefs. If we are coming from a point of addiction, whether that be to pornography or any substance or activity (this includes being addicted to the drama that our pain creates around us), then observing our beliefs will begin to stir things up.

Our beliefs serve the purpose of protecting us from the full realization of what we are medicating—the trauma and pain that lie deep within us all. Like scaffolding holding up a structure, our beliefs prevent the bandages and stitches covering all of our unresolved pain and repressed emotion from unraveling.

The reality is, this is going to be very uncomfortable and difficult. Accept that.

As Tom Hanks' character Jimmy Dugan says in the film *A League of Their Own*: "It's supposed to be hard. If it wasn't hard, everyone would do it. The *hard* is what makes it great." If you want freedom, you are going to have to step past that part of you that simply wants to avoid conflict within yourself and with the people around you, seeking a peace that can be more easily understood as "the absence of conflict."

In my case, and in Dave's, we had to be more concerned with *what works* than what we *believed to be factually true* about the universe.

I'm a Christian, but my faith in Christ is not dependent on the historical accuracy of the Gospels, but rather in the experience of freedom and the touch of grace on my life as I seek a deeper experience of God through a life spent walking the path I understand Jesus points toward. And in my Christian belief, I realize these ideas apply to any belief regarding addiction. Even the beliefs you may gain from this book are only true if they motivate you to take action toward forsaking the prison you live in.

The anxiety of trying to find the correct or right belief will follow you like a shadow—always there, never dissipating. You'll always have to be better, do better, know more, try harder. It is simply a matter of how much suffering you choose to endure and how severe your circumstances become before you are ready to lay anything and everything down to find actual freedom. Many people take it all the way to their deathbed before suddenly seeing a light that gives them just a glimpse of what could have been. Some even take it to the grave with them.

But, in the end, if you want freedom in this life and the joy and peace that Jesus seemed to indicate was available, then you must ask some very difficult questions of the deepest parts of yourself. If you want to be free—if you really want to be free—then you *must* engage your beliefs in a new way.

In Brightest Day, In Blackest Night...

My favorite superheroes are all colored green. As I write this, I am sitting in a coffee shop in my hometown wearing a green t-shirt with the logo of none other than Hal Jordan, otherwise known as the Green Lantern. Why?

The central discussion of the Green Lantern universe is this: What is the most powerful force in the universe? Some would say love and others would say the human spirit. I guess in current American culture, some would say advertising. In any case, Green Lantern lore says that at the beginning of all that is, the Guardians learned to harness the most powerful energy in the world, the green energy of *will*. That is, the will to *do* something was *the* thing that could change everything. The next most powerful force? That would be the yellow energy of *fear*. In other words, the yellow energy keeps you from doing something and the green energy gets you to do something.

That's why I wear this t-shirt. Because when my life began to change was when I finally gained the will (or perhaps *courage* would be a more fitting word) to *do* something. In my case, as in so many, it was suffering that drove me to this point.

Think about it: you may think you've done something about your addiction. You may have bought some software, gone to an accountability group or some twelve-step meetings, or maybe done one of those fasts from whatever it is you think is your problem. You might have done those things and they might have helped or they might not have, but you still don't feel free. You might have even done those things and are in active sobriety, not currently using porn or drugs or alcohol, but you can still feel it; you aren't free and you know this because freedom is a *feeling* produced by a state of reality.

So the question becomes: why haven't you done something different? One friend of mine recently told me that he simply didn't know what to do. I get that. He was told or not told something and believed or didn't believe these things, so there exists inside of him a *belief* that there simply isn't anything he can do. And this is where the green energy of will and the yellow energy of fear come into play. Why do some people have the will to continue to fight and search and grind until they find freedom and some don't? Some people don't move and have no idea why; some people forsake everything to break free. There are countless stories about people who found true freedom, so there has always been a way there, as well as people willing to show us that way, but the beliefs we hold have kept us from those stories, perhaps because some of the people who tell these stories are more focused on capitalizing on people's pain than healing it.

The Three Elements of Belief
There are three elements to belief, and understanding them is key in this process of finding freedom. In this chapter,

we'll tackle the first one: What you believe. The next chapter will take us beyond belief and look at why we believe things and then most importantly, what function your beliefs perform in your life.

Many people, both religious and non-religious, are prepared to openly explain the first element: what they believe. They hold a dogmatic belief about everything from God to frozen yogurt and often see these beliefs as the most important aspect of their lives. They structure their lives to uphold, defend, and affirm those beliefs—from what books to read and entertainment to listen to and watch, to religious services and political affiliations. I have had more than a few people tell me that exploring my belief systems by stepping outside of traditional boundaries is dangerous. For them, doubt and uncertainty are to be feared, a belief structure (in which I was raised) that calls any doubt of traditional evangelical doctrines a "Spirit of Unbelief."

A few out there are able to articulate the second element—*why* they believe what they believe. Most often, people I've discussed this with say they were simply taught what to believe. There is usually a reference to upbringing and parents and churches, or the lack thereof.

Very few people tackle the third element, the doorway to freedom. It is extremely common for it to take a tremendous amount of suffering for people to engage the question of "what function do our beliefs perform in our lives?" Usually, there is a realization at a conscious level that looks something like this: my beliefs have failed me. I asked my beliefs to free me and give me the abundant life that my heart longs for, and they haven't. If what I believe is true, then why am I not free? What am I missing?

Let's have a closer look at these elements of belief so we can more clearly lay out the road to freedom on this Sacred Journey.

Deep...ish - WHAT we believe

As I currently sit here typing this, I am wearing jeans, the aforementioned Green Lantern t-shirt, and a well-known brand of shoes. Even these simple facts are enough to tell you something about what I believe. The whole Green Lantern thing aside, the manufacturer of jeans I am wearing has been accused in the not-too-distant past of human rights violations in their factories in Southeast Asia, as have the manufacturers of my shoes. I *know* these things to be true and I "believe" that child labor and worker abuse is wrong......don't I?

It's the difference of *knowing* something and *knowing that we know* something. When we hear reports about child labor in the factories that produce practically every product we consume here in the West, we know they are true, but we don't want to know that we know because then we might feel obligated to do something about it. This knowledge of our knowledge would begin to unravel our sense of ourselves as good people with good intentions and good hearts.

So, we just keep typing and attempt to keep the anxiety of our threatened identities at bay. (...he writes as he slowly sips another cup of Starbucks coffee...)

It is safe to say that what people believe is as diverse as people themselves, though there are plenty of groups who crowd around a belief that they share, like political movements, social justice ideas, creeds, or a belief the Mariners will win the World Series this year (which they won't, and we all know this deep down). Believing is a byproduct of living and like I said before, it is somewhat like breathing. As we live and breathe and experience our lives, belief is a way of organizing those experiences into something we can understand and identify with.

What we believe often reveals what questions we are willing to ask and what questions remain in the darkness and rooted in our pain. And going deeper can begin to ditch all the guilt and shame that so inhibits our ability to see clearly enough to really pursue freedom.

When we use pornography (or other types of "drugs"), it is because *some part* of us believes this is the best thing for us. *Some part* of us believes this thing will give us what we *need* at the deep levels. For instance, the use of pornography can be, and usually is, much deeper than the need for a sexual "release." The unconscious self seeks the deeper fulfillment of a need: the need to be accepted and loved in all its idiosyncrasies. The drive to fulfill our deepest needs is why we make the choices we make. It is the darkness within us that wants us to believe that this is not a choice we are making at some level of our consciousness. Like the Agents in the *Matrix* films, who spend a great deal of words on trying to convince the humans that choice is an illusion and love is a myth, our pain would like us to keep getting that next hit so we can keep living under the belief that this is best for us. There is a Mr. Anderson inside of every Neo. And the key question asked in those philosophical treatments is this: do we actually possess the ability to choose or not?

You're reading this book because something inside you believes there is some truth waiting for you in a place you have never been before; that there is something *new*. You may have some sort of nagging thought that God just might have some real power and that Jesus wasn't just wagging his tongue about this power that lies within us all. So, as far as the importance of what you believe, put it in the aquarium and take a step back.

For our purposes here, you get to take a vacation from thinking your beliefs are anything more than a signal flare sent by something deeper inside of you screaming to get out...and a stepping stone into the deeper questions: why do you believe what you believe and what function do your beliefs perform in your life?

chapter 6
THE PURPOSE OF BELIEF

Most people, when asked the question as to why they believe something, give simple answers like, "It was what I was taught," or they have a story they want to relate about an experience that changed their beliefs in some tangible way. A few will say, "I don't know," but that's usually something that takes a series of questions to get to. Like a type of "question staircase," we can get ourselves to the edge of our conscious world very fast by asking why we believe things and then following the answers. No matter what answer you have for why you use pornography (or any other substance or behavior) to medicate your unconscious pain, following the behavior inward is the key. When I was an addict, my staircase was relatively short and it would have looked somewhat like this:

You: Hey Seth, why do you use pornography?

Seth: I think it is just a struggle every guy has. We're sinful people and we have our battles to fight.

You: Why do you believe you are sinful?

Seth: Because I do sinful things. Everyone sins. That's why we need a savior.

You: But you believe in Christ as your savior. You believe you are a new creation. So why do you keep doing the same thing and why do you feel so guilty about everything if you're forgiven?

Seth: (Shame and guilt being triggered and eyes moving downward) I don't know, man. I just don't know. (Perhaps some cussing or tears would begin at this point.)

It didn't take long before I hit the "I don't know" stage. I might have started talking about eternity and how we will all know it all in the "sweet by and by," but every addict eventually gets to "I don't know" if they follow the questions down the staircase. Then we are left standing at a crossroads that can take us to freedom. When we forsake a demand for certainty and satisfaction in our own intellect, we can begin to learn something *new*.

Here's the catch though: if having all the answers, certainty, and concrete ideas are the goal of every search, *then freedom is always a ways off.* When I ask, "Why do you believe what you believe?" and your answer is something akin to "The Bible says so" or "God says so" or "Because it is true," then what more can be said? I've had plenty of people, especially religious ones, tell me there is no point in discussing these things because there is no common ground to stand on (theologically and doctrinally speaking), which guarantees we remain addicts in one form or another. One thing for sure is that it is a difficult place to live, this space where certainty and addiction are forced to be bedfellows, which is an extremely common occurrence. Addiction signals a resounding "*I don't know!*" at the heart of our conscious life. If you are unable to utter those three terrifying words "I don't know," then despite your beliefs and desires, you are not truly seeking freedom. Which is why you haven't found it. You're seeking answers and certainty and a belief in freedom.

I've found that actual freedom lies in the mystery.

Deeper still — WHAT FUNCTION Do My Beliefs Serve in My Life?

My buddy Sam is way into flashlights. He has an amazing collection of them and sometimes we go to the cabinet just to look at all his flashlights. Where he sees a deep commitment to technology and illumination, I see a bunch of flashlights. I think, *I could really use a flashlight in my truck*, while he thinks about what planet he could hit with that beam. I don't understand it, but I do admire his commitment to illumination.

I am a philosopher by nature and people like me believe questions are flashlights. One of the brightest of those flashlights is: "What function do my beliefs perform in my life?" Since addiction lies within our deepest parts, lingering in the shadows of our unconscious pain, then we must shine this light into the pain that exists in the dark corners of our souls.

Sometimes this is a scary thing—like a horror movie where some poor sap goes into the dark shed out back to investigate a noise. We all know he shouldn't go there, but he does anyway because he *has* to find the truth. He goes alone, of course, with a small flashlight with far too little illumination (Sam would recommend the t-492 for its variable brightness settings, plus it can double as a club). He pans the flashlight, right to left for effect, when suddenly that really nasty thing jumps out at him. It probably eats him, and the makers of that film count on the fear their characters relay and their audience experiences to be the thing that gives the scene its horrifying effect.

If the character just stood his ground and with one punch, destroyed the evil thing, we as the audience would find it oddly empowering (and perhaps disappointing) to think a person doesn't have to be afraid. That's called authority. Jesus taught that our spirits have a great deal of authority, if only we could see it and learn how to use it.

Asking certain questions can lead us to the authority and power we hold dormant in our spirits. Reflecting on our beliefs, shining a light on them, and observing them starts to crack that door open. Then through that authority, we are empowered to be healed.

When I was an addict, my beliefs had no power unto themselves beyond giving me some sort of psychological direction one way or another. Coming to believe that every man endured this battle was helpful for me psychologically. It normalized things, letting me know that I wasn't alone in this struggle. But it didn't transform anything beyond my own psychology, which can be powerful when it motivates a person towards action. But if all it does is create more belief, then its operative power is again disconnected from any actual change.

The Energy of Beliefs

As any psychologist will tell you, changing your internal belief systems can provide a shift in your life. When a person comes to the understanding of how an unhealthy belief has been dominating their life, that *self-awareness* can assist a person in developing more helpful behaviors.

Porn addiction is an obvious example of this. Understanding what you are medicating with pornography would be coming to a greater self-awareness. But self-awareness, which is a collection of beliefs about yourself, doesn't heal the wound.

A recent example from my life has been the intersection of my love for American football while deploring the brain-injury crisis that is coming more and more into the light. I always knew the sport was dangerous, but I didn't want to know just how dangerous or even be confronted with the knowledge I already possessed. I didn't want to see the tears of the widows or mothers who have lost sons, because then I would be confronted with needing to act. My pain doesn't want me to sacrifice my unconscious desires. It would much rather have its desires and pretend everything is all right, especially because it is often so difficult to know what to do about it.

Another incredibly tough example is the everyday issue of panhandling. I live in Seattle, and every day I drive by someone on an overpass holding a sign asking for money or a job or food or some other kind of help. It is fascinating to observe myself internally when faced with this flesh and bone reality.

First come the rapid fire, almost unconscious basic questions in a matter of seconds: What do I do? They obviously need help—but is $5 from my wallet going to help? Maybe. Probably not. Will they just buy something that contributes to an addiction? Maybe. Maybe not. Should I do something? What can I do? I have a busy life—so much to do, and bills to pay myself. Argh!

Then comes the internal shutdown: I feel almost nothing. Don't make eye contact. Chest is getting a little tight. Do I look at them? Don't look at them. Drive byyyyy......phew. Unconsciously erase them from memory. Reboot.

I have always found it interesting how hard I seek a system of control/belief to help me with those moments. If I can just have a program that I can run through — a set belief system about all of those poor people who are dying on the inside as they stand there with their cardboard signs — then I could escape this unconscious knowledge that in the world I *claim* to be trying to bring about, people wouldn't have to get so creative with cardboard and sharpies.

All these examples are to make the point that *what* we believe consciously often times is nothing more than a mask or a shield to protect us from what we believe sub-consciously. Or put another way, what we believe is protecting us from what we *actually* believe. It is this function that we must become conscious of and begin to understand.

All You Gotta Do is Believe

I became a father one year ago at the time of this writing, and watching my daughter develop her sense of reality fascinates me. My wife is a Mental Health Specialist for children; she explained to me how my daughter's current sense of security is very dependent on, of all things, my face. To illustrate: Let's say my daughter goes to pet a puppy. The puppy seems harmless until, suddenly and without warning, it snaps at her face with a growl and a bark. My daughter would jump back quickly with a start and immediately look to my face for reassurance that she's okay, and also to gauge whether or not she should be afraid. My face can hold for her the felt experience of strength and comfort and reassurance, or it can hold panic, fear, anger, pain, and even shame.

Through these cues, my daughter can develop a sense of either "Be afraid, be very afraid" or "Don't sweat the small stuff." These instances can create lasting trauma or just be a scary incident that leads to wisdom for future situations. And that's just an instance with a dog. More impactful are the ways I shame her or threaten her with my face whenever she makes a mistake and I am triggered. These moments seemingly try to present themselves every-day in multiple ways.

This is how we form belief. What we believe about God, the world, other people, and ourselves is developed not only through the deep and personal direct relationship between parents and their children, but also through interactions with everyday people and events. As we mentioned earlier, belief is a way of organizing these events into a system that teaches us how to function in the world.

All of this, if honestly approached, should hopefully lead you to the conclusion that it is time to take the questions of what you believe and why to a deeper level: naming the function of your beliefs. If we are deal-ing with addiction of any sort, the knowledge that your beliefs are powerless to heal you and transform you and also the knowledge that the power we seek is an altogether separate thing from the belief in that power is incredibly important.

Curiosity and Courage

So if addiction is the execution of a belief system we hold at a sub-conscious level, then the important question about things like porn addiction is not "What are you doing?" but "What function is it performing?" As we said before, porn isn't the problem; it's medication for the problem. So, if the operative question is "What are you medicating?" the staircase begins and it will plunge into the depths quickly and powerfully. It takes a tremendous amount of curiosity and courage to descend those steps.

The good news is that you have that courage within you, contained in your spirit. My goal is to show you how to use that unbelievably powerful tool. In the gospels, Jesus told his followers they would do greater things than him. I like to think he said it with a wink and smile, with a parenthetical "If you could see what I see" or "If you have the guts" preceding the statement. In this courageous exploration, you will undoubtedly find things you didn't know were there—I know I did. You will likely find pain, trauma, anger, and many other things. In other words, you will find your humanity.

Chapter 7
TRIGGERS

One word that needs to be adopted as we form a language that allows us to find some freedom is the word "trigger." If you have done some therapy, read a few therapeutic books, or been on the right websites, you may have heard the word before. Many people in the world of addiction use the word when referring to someone's addiction being triggered.

For instance, when I was an addict, fighting hard to bounce my eyes from every sexually stimulating image in my culture, my addiction would get triggered from things like commercials or billboards with sexual imagery. I would start to feel the numbness set in and I would begin to dissociate, which is a psychological term that basically describes a person consciously separating from themselves. My guilt and shame would fall asleep for a bit and I would be driven to take the trigger to the end release. Then, after another 30 minutes or so, my body would begin to wake back up and reconnect to my consciousness, and I would begin the routine of feeling guilt and shame about what I had done. That would continue for a time until the whole cycle started again.

But, when I use the word "trigger" in the context of this book, *I mean something different entirely.* Using the same example as above, what was actually being triggered was the pain that demanded the medication inside my sub-conscious. It was the same thing that would trigger when I would interact with my wife. Even being in her presence would sometimes cause an indescribable rage to rise up inside of me. It was the most raw form my pain would take. At the time, I would blame her and identify the anger as a part of who I was. What was actually happening was that the pain that I had residing in the deepest parts of my subconscious, repressed deep in my body, was being lit like a match. Even when I wasn't triggered, I could still feel the pain inside. For me, it manifested as butterflies in my stomach almost constantly, what is often diagnosed as "anxiety." It was pain waiting to be triggered, packed down like gunpowder inside my body from a very young age.

Obviously, relationships—and the issues that arise in relationships, such as financial issues or personality con-flicts, are the most prominent examples of triggers. Sports and work are other great examples. An easily understood example is road rage. You make a little slip in your lane change on the freeway and now you have a maniac chasing you down and trying to kill you (or perhaps you *are* the maniac). What is happening inside this person to make them so angry? It had very little to do with our lane change. But while we can see *this* trigger quite plainly, we often fail to see it in *ourselves*. Sometimes we are given tools in our lives that can be very helpful for showing us our pain, and it is awareness of these tools that we aim to enhance.

My dog was a very useful tool when this all started because when he would do something like pee on the carpet despite my efforts to train him, I felt a disproportionate rage rise up inside me. After all, he's a dog. He wasn't trying to tick me off; he was acting on instinct. He would do what dogs do and I would react like he was living in sheer rebellion, his only goal to disrespect me. One time, I body-slammed him on the ground for biting me on the hand, screaming, "*Don't you ever bite me again!*" as if he had suddenly learned English. I felt out of control. Serves me right for trying to pull a piece of rotten chicken out of his mouth, even if he did get it out of the garbage. I stepped back in that moment and started to ask myself what was going on inside of me. Where did *that* come from?

It took me many years to be able to clearly see that when my wife "made" me angry, even when I felt justified, I was being triggered. It was *always* something deeper inside of me—It wasn't her. (It turns out that there is some real truth to the phrase, "It's not you. It's me.") This isn't to say she doesn't have things that need to change within her, but those things weren't relevant to the change that needed to happen within *me*.

And then came the baby. It turns out that sleep deprivation combined with any current stress is a wonderfully powerful trigger. Kids in general are just an amazing trigger because they touch all of our deepest stuff. On an unconscious level, we recognize what happened to us when we were that age and we often simply repeat these things, even when we don't want to.

I know this might be difficult to grasp, and you might resist the idea that negative emotions indicate something deeper is being triggered. We are often so sure the person we are associating the negative emotions with is out to get us. And they may be...but that doesn't change the fact that we are still being triggered. When that emotion comes up, if we could stop in that moment and ask, with a genuine curiosity, what that emotion actually is (to the point where we even pinpoint the physical sensation that it brings and where that sensation is located in our bodies), it would have the effect that our trusty flashlight has on darkness. And, as it says in the New Testament, the darkness cannot comprehend that light.

So, as a practical step, I am going to attempt to trigger you, or I should say *you* are intentionally going to attempt to trigger yourself, and we are going to use language to do so. It is best to do this in a safe, quiet place where you can be alone (a parked car away from onlookers works well).

Intentionally accessing emotions or repressed pain inside you can cause surprising reactions at times. It can shock others or even frighten them to see someone who is feeling their pain and not holding it back. When I first began to do this, I would at times feel an intense need to scream, cry, or even throw up, so when I felt those things, I simply allowed them to happen. Your body and spirit understand how to heal you and what to do with negative emotions. But there is a part of you that will try to resist feeling and releasing emotion. Be prepared. This is only a precursor to the practices that we will discuss later.

Step 1—Identify What Triggers You

Think carefully about the things that make you angry, that tempt you to cry, or that cause you to shut down. Your goal is to trigger some of those things, so if you have tools you would like to use, feel free. Music can be very helpful for triggering emotion, or even movies. Before I was able to expel the suppressed grief I had around my father's death (he died when I was 12), movies like *Field of Dreams* and *The Lion King,* which portrayed father/son relationships and the issues surrounding loss of these relationships, *killed* me. I would spend tremendous amounts of energy trying to hold back the tidal wave of pain they triggered. Over the years, I had unconsciously learned how to breathe and clench my abs and jaw until I went numb and would immediately go that default whenever that pain would be triggered. I wish I had understood that those films could act as agents of healing and just let it flow.

A quick note on emotion: I know there are those of you who can't feel *anything.* Your emotions are pushed down so deeply that it's hard to believe you even have them. I have been sitting with a friend whose pain manifests this way, and as he has begun to see that *not feeling* is not the way he wants to live, he has begun to sense his pain rising to the surface. But he doesn't want to start to feel it—he's scared to death that if he breaks down those walls keeping his emotions at bay, he'll have no defenses from his wife's rage or his son's tantrums. This is an authentic fear and it must be respected. Attempting to change your life and resurrect your spirit is no small thing. If he decides to go down that road, he will need help. Luckily, we have each other and can help each other out when needed. There are wonderful therapeutic tools out there and we will discuss many of them—and they could all help both my friend and you. But my friend can also stay the way he is and just survive if he chooses. That's okay—it's his life and his choice.

On to the feeling.

You might just sit quietly and recall an incident—a fight with your spouse/mother/father/child/sibling/boss or a moment of extreme anxiety—the trigger will often be accompanied by a physical sensation. Something as basic as determining what causes you stress can be helpful. The physical sensation is very important: a little bit like a bread-crumb trail we can use to observe what is going on inside you. In my case, at some point along the journey, I was *deeply* triggered by hearing certain preachers lay guilt and shame at people's feet. It caused a pain in my chest and sparked an intense rage. It also manifested inside of me as judgment towards those men, and I desired to be free from that. So...what I did with that was...

Step 2—*Intentionally Trigger Your Pain*

We must do this with an intention of *observation only*. For instance, don't intentionally start a fight with your spouse if they are the only thing presently triggering you. But, understand that if your partner is a trigger at this point along the journey, and in that moment when that trigger happens (they say *that thing* in *that way* and you feel *that emotion*), if you can observe it as a trigger and honestly ask the question of what is *actually* being triggered, you will be taking the first steps down the path that leads to freedom.

From my story, even recently, I have intentionally listened to sermons from some of the aforementioned preachers I deeply disagree with and even find poisonous. When I've done this, I have often found deep anger within, and triggering this anger has allowed me to observe it and ask God what I am dealing with. This does not always result in some deep revelation of repressed pain or dark stuff inside of me, but it does teach me to distinguish between healthy anger and pain that needs to exit the body.

This is where language will begin to show itself as the barrier that it is. For instance, if you are an Evangelical Christian, listen to a talk by someone at the opposite end of the spectrum. If you are on that other end of the spectrum or aren't religious at all, listen to some fundamentalist preaching or talk radio that makes you nuts. It's the language that will ignite the fuse. The taboo issues—politics and religion—are great for this. This is why they are taboo. They arouse repressed energies within us that we spend a tremendous amount of time, money, and energy keeping pushed down inside of us.

Step 3—Feel the Trigger

This is much harder than you think. Your pain does not want to be noticed or have any light shed on it. Your mind will have a hard time trying not to control it. But, if you can simply feel what is being triggered for 60 seconds in an observational mode, you will have made progress and possibly learned something new about yourself. Locate the feeling in your body. Where does it sit and how does it manifest? Tightness in your chest perhaps? Knots in your stomach? Even if this is not new or difficult for you, there is a next step to take—there is always another trigger to go after.

I was attempting to help a friend of mine the other day with this. I just asked him to close his eyes, stop thinking for a minute, and just feel the burning in his stomach that he had complained about. He couldn't stop thinking for even thirty seconds, but he recognized this fact. He asked me, "I wonder why I can't just feel that thing in my stomach when I want to?" Great question. Even this morsel of curiosity and knowledge was a step in the right direction.

I have coached soccer for well over a decade now and this method has been incredibly helpful for me as I try to get the best out of my players. One of the great things about sports is that failure is inevitable. Often, when my players fail, even in small ways, they get triggered. I have players who will fly off the handle at a referee, opponent, teammate, or even me. I have players who will shut down and stop playing. Whatever is being triggered inside these athletes is enough to kill their potential not only to perform well, but also to enjoy the sport they are playing.

One particular team I coached a few years back had this effect on me in a way I had never before (and have not since) encountered. They were 13-year-old girls, and their parents were just as addicted to drama as they were. So, my job to get everyone on the same page and working together to produce results on the field was a difficult one. The toughest part was that I couldn't go out there and play the games myself; I just had to stand there and take the failure. I still regret some of the things I said to those players and their parents when I was triggered by their constant underperformance. It got ugly at times.

I spend a great deal of time with triggered players now, teaching them to feel. Even this morning, before I sat down to write, I trained a 14-year-old soccer player one-on-one. He was struggling with a certain skill and the failure triggered him. I brought him in, asked him to take a deep breath and describe to me what he was feeling.

"I'm feeling mad," he said.

"Mad is a secondary feeling. You *are* obviously experiencing anger, but what are you actually feeling? In your body?"

He had to sit with that for a while. I told him to breathe. He started taking deep breaths. I helped him with it a bit. "Are you feeling numb? Pain? Butterflies? In your stomach? Chest?"

He stood there breathing for a bit and then said, "Oh. There it is. I feel a hole in my chest." He pointed. "It's right here."

Later on, his awareness of the feeling became more acute; he felt two things, with one surrounding the other. He could feel the outer layer more, but the one underneath was larger. I simply explained to him that there were suppressed emotions inside of him and what that meant.

"That's why you're struggling to improve," I told him. "Whatever that is, it's shutting you down and disconnecting you from yourself whenever you are under threat of losing. Losing is inevitable. We have to find a way to deal with that."

That's as far as I took it at that moment. Oftentimes, triggers need to be approached a little bit at a time, because we can be talking about something that has been with us for a long time. It is no small thing to decide to deal with these repressed emotions and pain. It is also life-transforming.

So, as we move forward, feel what's going on inside of your body. Monitor the triggers. If something comes up inside of you, maybe butterflies or the "hole" in the chest, or a pain in your back or a tingling in your hands, place your hand over it and ask, "What is this?"

This is the beginning of the process...

Chapter 8
SEEING

I want you to take a moment and think of *The Matrix* films.
(If you haven't seen them, at least go watch the first one,
because it's a great movie—also, skip the rest of this
paragraph.) When Neo gets shot at the end of the first film
and then wakes up, he sees the world very differently: the
digital world around him suddenly becomes evident. He
sees the Matrix for what it really is. Because his surrounding reality is no longer hidden, he ceases to be afraid of
it and instead changes the rules that seem to bind his
fellow humans.

It is no coincidence that, upon the release of *The Matrix*
in 1999, a large chunk of the population in America drew a
Jesus-parallel with Neo. As described in the gospels, Jesus
seemed to be able to bend and even break the rules when
he laid hands on people and healed them and chased evil

spirits out of people with a calm authority, not unlike Neo stopping bullets in mid-air.

There will be some who would respond to that last sentence with a simple, "Yeah, but he was God." Jesus rendered the debate moot with the statement made to his disciples in John 14:12, where he explained that those who "believed" in him would do the same works that he was doing and beyond. He said they would do *greater* works than him (and he raised people from the dead!). As far as I'm concerned, that statement leads to some of the deepest and most important questions a human being can ask. It forces us to face the simple yet *incredibly* complex question: "What did Jesus mean by 'believe?'"

There are obviously plenty of people who believe Jesus was the Son of God, myself included, and also plenty who claim that belief to be the core of their spiritual and practical life. But if you're carrying the deep burden of pornography addiction or depression or the myriad anxiety issues you may be carrying, then one of the key examinations you must do in this process as we live inside the larger question regarding belief and what actual power it has is this: What did Jesus see that we don't?

If you could see what I see

First, we must differentiate between "seeing" and "believing." Whereas many religious people would understand believing to be something that *can* be done without seeing or experiencing (many interpretations of the word "faith" would ascribe to a concept that has been traditionally labeled "blind" faith), the kind of faith described by Jesus is a *reality* that is *seen*.

When Jesus told Thomas "blessed are those who have not seen and still believed," he was speaking of Thomas living with a closed heart. His friends were telling stories of hope about Jesus' resurrection, but Thomas couldn't believe their testimonies. They came, shouting, "We have seen the Lord!" and Thomas essentially said, "Unless I see him, it can't be true." His heart was closed to the idea that it could be true and thus closed to the testimony his friends were speaking. I can imagine Peter standing there saying to Thomas, "Bro... are you calling me a liar? Why would I lie to you?"

Just as in John 3, when Jesus tells Nicodemus that "we testify to what we have seen and you do not accept our testimony", *we unconsciously ignore the implications of the stories* we see and hear, each of which has an inherent implication for *our* story. For instance, the stories my brother and I have told about our freedom from addiction have implications for your story.

And yet, when I have told the outcome of my story to people, I have received a shocking amount of responses in the neighborhood of "I don't buy it" or "That can't happen;" even though I was much like the blind man whom Jesus had healed, just shouting my gratitude from the mountaintops, many of the people who heard me were more concerned with what my doctrines were than what I experienced. It was very confusing.

Believing without sight isn't convincing yourself something is real when you've never experienced it. It's being able to hear the story of a friend and explore it with honesty. If there is truth in it, that will be made evident eventually, but we close ourselves to the work of the Spirit, which is meant to lead us into truth, when we hang on to dogmatic ideas instead of listening to the stories that tell us of the ways we could be made whole.

They believed without seeing

There are plenty of examples of spiritual teachers and amazing individuals who lived with what seemed like an ability to see something your average Joe doesn't. Sacred texts are filled with them, while in our own lifetime, people like Mother Teresa saw the divine in every dying person, where most of us see beggars. Nelson Mandela saw a free South Africa when many saw hopelessness or violence. Martin Luther King, Jr's dream was a vision he held in his mind and articulated as well as any leader in history; that vision was obviously not in the minds of everyone who heard his "I Have a Dream" speech. Some seers accomplish "great" things we all learn about; others simply live in peace. This type of seeing is the central focus of many faith traditions, especially where Jesus walked.

Jesus was conscious of something we aren't. Not only did he articulate some of these mysteries to his twelve disciples as recorded in the Gospels, but the things he said and did have earned a particularly epic place in the human consciousness. When he healed the desperate souls who followed him everywhere, dragging disease, poverty, and pain along with them, he often used these words: "Your faith has made you well." These people seemed to possess nothing but the courage to be open to the implications of what Jesus did and said. If you were unable to walk your entire life and someone came to your village and said they had seen some guy heal a crippled person, what would you do?

In 2004, I visited the war-torn, southern part of Sudan (this was before South Sudan became an independent nation) with a medical team, and word quickly spread about the arrival of a group of Americans with food and medicine. It wasn't long before those with the faith to investigate that story started showing up at our camp. One man was carried over 15 miles on a stretcher by his four friends because he believed he could find healing if he could just get to us.

That is faith: courage to see that every story in every time and in every place has implications for our own story. That is the ability to see what Jesus saw, if even a tiny fraction of it. So, again, we have the question: what if we could see what Jesus saw? What would it be like to be completely aware of God? To know where God resides in, around, and through all things. What would it be like to be "God-Conscious?"

When I was a child, I always wondered what might happen if I took those 3-D glasses from the movie theater out into the world—maybe I could see things the way angels did. I actually thought this. Today, I sometimes like to picture Jesus walking around, handing people those 3-D glasses so they can see what He saw, then they would believe and be healed. He would often use a phrase in conjunction with his teaching: "He who has the eyes to see, let him see. He who has the ears to hear, let him hear."

Again, Jesus called this combination of sight and belief "faith." Even if you haven't seen with your physical eyes, your spirit is aware, and that awareness acts as an illuminating agent inside of you. As it says in the Gospel of John, the light shines in the darkness and the darkness cannot comprehend the light. This is what is so significant about the phrase "Your faith has made you well." Another way to say it would be, "Your light has illuminated the darkness you've carried." It can very quickly cause a peace to settle into the center of a person. Those darker elements that exist inside us begin to be uncovered and driven from their hiding places—and we experience this evacuation physically.

This conception of faith can help us understand why authority and faith are inextricably linked. Darkness of any kind, and that includes addiction, is rendered powerless in the light. Let's call this event "awakening." Awakening can be accompanied by healing events like what my brother and I experienced, but no matter how one encounters it, awakening always involves a reorientation of oneself to the world.

Night Vision

Not too long ago, a large insurance company aired a television commercial that featured two very happy antelopes as the main characters. They were happy because they had somehow acquired night vision goggles. The commercial consisted of them mocking a lion named Carl for his attempts to stalk them.

"Look who's back."

"Again?"

"It's embarrassing."

"Totally embarrassing."

"We can see you Carl!"

"We can totally see you!"

"Have you thought about going vegan, Carl?"

They say these things without a trace of fear.

This is like that. In fact, "I see you" has become one of the most powerful verbal tools I have used in rooting out the darkness and pain in my own life. When we begin to look inside with that understanding—or even an attempt to understand things that way—things begin to happen. It is the first step of the path to a freedom most people have never experienced.

So, using that interpretive lens, what if we took some of Jesus' teachings and added this idea: "If you could see what I see." As you read these, remove the behavioral reading and think instead about Jesus showing you the Matrix, much like Neo's phone conversation at the end of the first film. Neo's new vision gives him the passion and license to go and teach the world a new way of seeing.

You're worried about the bills again—perhaps there are knots in your stomach or pain in your chest as you think about how you're going pay them. Jesus throws his arm over your shoulder, points out the window, and says, "See those flowers out there, how they are dressed? See that tree, how large and strong it is? It's been there in that place, patient and still, waiting for this moment for you to see the beauty in it. If you could see what I see, you wouldn't worry about what you're going to eat or what you're going to wear, because you would fully understand that, like this tree, your heavenly Father knows what you need and loves you as his own child."

Peter begins to sink in the water when he becomes afraid of the huge waves. We can all relate to the fear of the unknown. Jesus leans down and takes his hand, saying, "Oh you of poor sight. If you could see what I see, you wouldn't have doubted. You would have run across the waves. Now rise and let me show you the way."

He even hinted at this idea in somewhat poetic terms in his conversation with Nicodemus. The religious leader came to him at night when Jesus described this idea of being "born again." Jesus was a Jew speaking to a fellow Jew—a scholar of the Torah—who was deeply confused. "Surely I tell you, the wind blows where it pleases and you don't know where it comes from and where it is going. So it is for everyone born of the spirit." Read another way, "You cannot see the wind, but you can see the effects of the wind. So it is with everyone who is born of the spirit. And you may not understand where this is coming from or where it is going. So have your eyes open. You will see the effects of the spirit of God that is within you." What are the effects of the spirit? We have spoken about them already: love, joy, peace, patience, kindness, goodness, faithfulness, gentleness, self-control. And I am saying that the fruits of the spirit include the end of addiction as well. There is no law of any kind that can stand against these things.

Where you see these things, you see the fingerprints of God.

Our Self-Awareness is Killing Us

Self-awareness, though a very necessary step towards taking actions that change your life, runs its course over time. You can hit a ceiling of sorts where you have no choice but to acknowledge that it has limitations. Knowing something in your mind is not consciousness. Awakening happens when the barrier gets broken between knowing something in your mind and knowing it in a way that transforms your soul. It is like there is a membrane that separates the two; it takes an experience to push through it. This is why even reading books like this can only get you so far unless you act. What you read might assist you in becoming more self-aware, but to transform your life and bring you into a deeper level of consciousness, your faith must make you well.

I had a friend who finally told me one day he was "sick and tired of being self-ware." He wanted freedom. He didn't want to feel the knots in his stomach, the rage in his chest, and the heaviness of sexual addiction anymore, no matter how much he understood it.

Another teacher/writer friend of mine—who anyone and everyone around him considers an enlightened individual who had it all together—told me, "I know this stuff I talk about gives me a certain measure of freedom...but I'm still miserable. I'm not happy and I don't know why." It seems that some suffering requires that kind of language to be properly understood.

What's the deal with Grace?

Most porn addicts I talk to have an answer when I ask them why they're addicted. They give me answers that range from theological discourses about sin and the pervasive-ness of evil to academic commentary on overly active sex drives. I have one friend who still believes it's just a fact of nature that his sex drive is just too intense. His wife would never be able to satisfy him, he says. And he means that well—no knock on his wife. He's had to formulate some answer to pacify the shame and guilt wrecking his insides.

St. Paul wrote that, "All things are permissible, but not all things are beneficial." That's grace—you can do whatever you want whenever you want to. But the damage you can do in that time is pretty amazing. Understand—I am not saying this isn't permissible. It's just damaging. My friend with the unquenchable sex-drive speaks of grace, and it's actually quite beautiful to see someone live into the meaning of grace even a little bit. When my friend indulges in this way, he's living into one portion of that grace. Where his unconsciousness rises, grace rises even further. And yet I can hear Jesus saying to him, "If you could see what I see, you would take grace to be the extreme power it is." He would grow tired of indulging in the unending acceptance and forgiveness of God and would start searching for a deeper power in his faith.

For those of us seeking freedom, grace acts as a squeegee of sorts. The window of our soul is so dirtied by guilt and shame that we can't even see well enough to ask the question, "Why do I do this?" with any real honesty and determination. But when grace settles into our core, where all the pain resides, it cleans off the guilt and shame and suddenly the window becomes clear. We can see the pain that drives us. We can approach God and our own spirits with honest questions and hope for transformation.

No matter what you've done, how many times you've done it, or what you're about to do, the grace of the Creator persists. You cannot escape it and you cannot destroy it. Even though you may not be experiencing it, you are loved and accepted no matter what and there is nothing you can do to change that. It's up to you whether you want to experience that love and be healed or not. You can continue to become self-aware or you can begin to use that knowledge by seeking awakening. It's just a matter of time until we come to the place where living with the knowledge of your struggles simply isn't good enough—you don't want to live with them anymore. In the addiction treatment world, they call this place "rock bottom." In the language of Jesus, this is the place where the ground has become "fertile."

The Imago Dei

This awareness is all a wonderful thing, but would be a moot point if there wasn't some ability we possessed to use it to our advantage. This is why this concept of the *Imago Dei*, a Latin term meaning "Image of God" is so important. The book of Genesis, the creation poem of the ancient Jewish and Christian traditions, speaks of humanity being created "in the image of God." Debates have raged ever since about what that entails for the human race, but I see this image directly reflected in Christ and in the concept of consciousness as it relates to authority. Our Divine nature empowers us to be free, since we carry the DNA of God.

Name one issue you wish were different and move towards it in your thoughts. It might be struggles with addiction, depression, or anxiety, or perhaps worries about money or stress at work. Allow the questions regarding the issue to set in and the emotions to rise. Understand that what lives underneath that question or emotion holds the key to your freedom. When you ask yourself "why do I worry about money?"—the answer is almost always deeper than you initially think or understand. Consciousness is being able to go beyond the pat-answers like "I've just always been that way" to locating that worry in the body (rather than in your job, for instance) and sitting patiently with any mysteries you find within you.

As you already have read, porn addiction was that great question for me. Why am I addicted? Why can't I stop? What is in this that I think I need? Accompanying this questioning were energies in my body that I could feel: knots in my stomach, tightness in my chest, aching in my back, and headaches. The questions would trigger the feelings and then the feelings would lead to deeper questions. What are these knots? Why do I feel like I want to throw up so much? Why do I feel numb after I use porn?

This is where meditation became an incredibly helpful tool for me because my thoughts were always trying to interrupt and control what was taking place. I learned how to breathe deeply and find silence. I invited God into that space, and as I did, I would come to a deeper awareness that God was already there and had been there the whole time. As I learned to step outside my thoughts, much like observing my beliefs in the aquarium, I was able to start asking more probing questions pertaining to those feelings in my body. I would place my hand over that area of my stomach where I would feel the knots and ask the Spirit, "What is this?" And then things began to happen, some of which I've already described. Essentially, I took the light of consciousness and shined it in. And, as I have previously stated, darkness cannot deal with light. When that light shines inward, consciousness rises and our eyes are opened.

This experience changed me forever. It's that simple and that unbelievably complex at the same time. But it must be understood that the simplicity and complexity of it all lies in the *practice* of these things. You must ask the questions, feel the feelings, do the meditation, and plunge into the darkness in order to experience healing.

I had to grow to understand that sometimes cracking open my unconscious pain can get a little messy. I felt things I hadn't felt before. Should you try this, you may find the same. Some people experience a rising joy and peace at the very same time they experience anxiety and emotions exploding out of them that have been living caged inside them for a long, long, time. One friend of mine who started down this road described it as the worst and best feeling he had ever had at the same time.

So, that being said, now's a good time to put down the book and take a deep breath. Try five minutes with your eyes

closed, breathing deeply from the stomach, and observing
your thoughts. Watch them come and go like traffic.

When those energies start to rise up in your body (in
the form of physical sensations), feel them, and then ask
the Spirit what they are. Simply put, pray. The feelings
will probably be familiar to you, though you may not have
approached them like this before. If it is helpful, put your
hand on that place in your body where the feeling resides
and say this prayer: "Show me what this is."

Breathe.

Feel.

Be still.

And if you can make it five minutes, try ten. If you can
make it ten, try fifteen.

You get the idea.

The Resistance is Rarely Televised

In my own story, the complexity came in the form of the
resistance I encountered within myself. Anyone who has
ever tried silent meditation before knows that just breathing and observing one's thoughts can be incredibly difficult.
The sensations you feel in your body are real, repressed
emotions and wounds you have carried for a long time,
much of which you may have no memory of because they
happened to you before you had the capacity to form words
around the experience (some call this "pre-verbal" trauma).
This type of pain exists inside all of us — it is part of what

is often called *the human condition.*

As young children, we learn to suppress our emotions very quickly and it is almost unavoidable that we are going to be left with damage done when we exit that developmental part of our life around 7 or 8 years old. For many of us, the damage continues after that age. Your pain will resist being dislodged because it is embedded as a part of your identity. It is not *who* you are, but rather who you *think* you are... and oftentimes who you think you've *always* been. We often explain our weaknesses this way: "That's just the way I've always been." This repressed pain is most certainly why the question regarding who we are is so complex for us humanoids. And this is why we ask things like our vocations to tell us who we are — which they are not capable of doing.

The resistance you may experience to any type of stillness and silence is very, very, important to pay attention to. It is a wrestling match we must be willing to engage in. If we can take back the silence inside of us five minutes and one breath at a time, we will start down a path that will wake us up and give us life, hope, and a deeper consciousness of everything that is.

chapter 9
SEXUALITY

For a book dealing with porn addiction, we haven't talked that much about sex. And we don't necessarily have to talk about the act of sex to address the issue of sex addiction. My brother Dave and I have had many talks over the years about this very subject, so I asked him to write down some of what he was thinking. For this chapter, it is best if you take your moral observations (like whether it is right to have sex outside of marriage) and lay them down for a time. You'll be able to pick it all up again when the chapter is over, but this chapter is not about the moral aspects of sex. It is about sexuality: what it is, what it isn't, and what it could be.

DAVE: There has recently been a spate of films about porn addiction produced in Hollywood. I recently watched one of them and I was aware of the irony: watching a movie that addresses sex addiction is something that most "sex addicts" can't or shouldn't do in their current state of consciousness lest it trigger their addictive behaviors and possibly send them spiraling out of control. The moving images of a man walking down the street, struggling with every woman showing a little leg, every lingerie ad plastered on the bus stop... that same guy could never watch a movie like the one he is in. Because the director *must* show what the guy is struggling with.

And since the latest results of religiously based as well as academic studies have shown that anywhere from half to three quarters of American men are at least mildly addicted to porn, inside and outside the church, then the film *Don Jon* has a peculiar audience dynamic. The viewer would have a student-like perspective rather than simply be entertained. They might ask themselves, "Am I learning something? Am I supposed to be learning something from this? Does the sex scene in which the porn addict is falling off the wagon turn me on or does it teach me something?"

It's a crazy space to be in. But at least the filmmaker is trying to do *something*. He has an agenda and like all art, it's only partly to make money. It's worth examining here. And it's worth asking deeper questions that are brought about through these films.

Don Jon

Don Jon was the brainchild of the talented actor Joseph Gordon-Levitt, who wrote, directed, and starred in it. The main character is Jon, and the film deals more with his search for intimacy than his porn addiction. In this story, porn is a character, a dispassionate antagonist, held in space only by Jon's limited knowledge of what a healthy relationship might look like.

Intimacy was never modeled for Jon, and it is assumed he has never really experienced it in the home he came from. His father, played brilliantly by Tony Danza, is a silver-backed, profane, Catholic chauvinist, and Gordon-Levitt deftly displays Jon's mixture of disdain and admiration for his father. Meanwhile, his mother is just waiting for grand-children, begging her son to find a woman.

The breaking point comes through Jon's relationships with two women. The first is the gorgeous woman, the princess who wants it all, Barbara, played by Scarlett Johansson. She uses her looks and sex appeal to try to shape Jon into the person she wants him to be. The second is an older woman named Esther, played by Julianne Moore, who attends a college class with Jon. We learn that Esther has known intimacy. Her husband and son both died in a car crash a year and a half prior to the events of the film. Through a combination of her brokenness and wisdom gained from a life of love and pain, she accepts Jon for who he is. She even encourages him to look at "better" porn, not the "crap he looks at on the internet." And then later she educates him about what sex is supposed to be, but not in a way that insults his previous experience. As the film's writer, Gordon-Levitt shows us what he feels sex is all about: the connection of two souls, getting lost in each other.

And the connection "cures" Jon of his addiction. He walks away from porn. He's found the greater thing. For good? Perhaps. He is beginning to see. But I don't think Jon's cure is the point Gordon-Levitt is trying to make.

Gordon-Levitt even draws a comparison in the middle of the film, revealing Johansson's character Barbara's obsession with romantic movies as an equivalent problem to Jon's allegiance to porn, which she denies adamantly, claiming it's not the same thing. After all, she claims, porn is sick. Romantic movies are beautiful.

And that's the voice we are accustomed to hearing underneath all the discussions about God's grace and love and forgiveness. No matter how much we come to understand the truth about why we do what we do, the voice whispering in the dark, especially from the shadowed corners of our religious institutions, is one of shame.

"Men who use porn are sick. Romantic movies show us what love is supposed to be like."

"If a man really loves a woman, he wouldn't use porn."

"Real love isn't even tempted by porn."

Yet, the whole time I watched the film, I wondered how Esther had the ability to accept porn as okay while Barbara saw it as sick? It just doesn't bother Esther at all. Is she just as sick? Is she faking it? Is it her pain and grief? How has she gained this lens that allows her to see Jon with no fear, shame, or burden of guilt?

How do you see Jon? And in turn, how do you see yourself? This is a key question.

Are you sick?

Are you a disgusting person?

Have you ever really loved another person?
Really connected?

Have you ever found yourself looking at a person and had the profound revelation that they understand you?

Do you know what real love is? And if you do, has that kept you from using porn? If not, then what does that mean about you and love? Does it mean that the love wasn't real?

Do you, porn-user, even have a right to say that you know what love is? Or what sex is? Or what sex should be?

Listen to the dialogue in your head. *Write it down.*

Now read what you wrote down. Close your eyes. Breathe. Can you feel the "truth" of your answer? *Do you know what*

I mean by "truth"? I ask you that for a specific reason so let me clarify what I mean:

When I am sad and someone says to me, "Are you sad?" I might say, "No, I'm not a sad person." What I mean by this is that I'm not usually sad. Or I don't want people to think of me as sad. But the *truth* of the moment is that yes, I am sad because I can feel the sadness inside me. In that moment, were I to close my eyes, I could tell you exactly where the sadness is in my body. I might say, "I have a lump in my throat" or "I feel sick to my stomach." This is what we can call our "emotional truth." The importance of understanding this can't be understated, because if we can't come to grips and admit to the emotional truth of any moment, then that emotion has to be subdued and repressed. The "lump in your throat" has to be shoved down, as it were. And where does it go?

It goes deeper. And deeper is harder to find. Harder to heal. And it does more damage.

So back to the question: Do you know what real love with another person is? Do you even have a right to say that? Take a moment to find the *emotional truth* of the question. Admit it. Say it out loud. Stay with it. And read on...

The Two Davids

Early in my married life I split in two. The part of me that wanted the "wrong" sexual things crept into the shadows while the part of me that wanted what was "right" stayed in the light of day. Deciding what was wrong sex versus what was right sex wasn't really a conscious process. It was gradual and came through a combination of what I was/wasn't taught about sex, what I was/wasn't taught about God, and what I was/wasn't taught about myself—all in my childhood. And it probably is safe to say there was an unhealthy dose of popular media and culture tossed into that mix. But what I dealt with media-wise *pales* in comparison to the generation coming up, with the average first exposure to internet porn currently being at the age of 11.

My wife noticed it early on in our marriage. At that time, I had never really looked at porn. But for me, sex was stressful because I felt an intense desire to "perform" correctly. It was difficult for me to accept that my body was sexually attractive in any way, but I could extol the virtues of her feminine figure for days. I couldn't even fathom someone finding me sexy.

In my upbringing, the Old Testament book *Song of Solomon* was upheld as *the* textbook for marital intimacy. Part of my childhood programming was that a man should be a gentle lover, *just* like King Solomon. So I spent most of my early marriage seeking to discover and understand my wife's sexuality, not my own. This is *extremely* important to examine because if you don't understand your own sexuality, you can't possibly understand someone else's.

Sexuality as Connection

Sexuality can be seen through an infinite number of lenses. Psychology, neuroscience, and most religious belief systems have a way of regulating how we view sex. For instance, a biologist, when asked to define sexuality, might deliver a science-based answer like, "Sexuality is the evolutionary instinct to mate so that a species can procreate and carry on its existence." A pastor might say, "Sexuality is the God-given gift of physical love between a man and a woman, with the ultimate aim of bringing children into the world and glorifying the Creator."

For the moment, we're going to take a different perspective. For our purposes, it's helpful to define our sexuality as the part of ourselves that connects us to everything, including God, ourselves, a life partner, and even nature. By this definition, sex is not a physical act at all but a spiritual state of being. Sex is not intercourse. In fact, sex has nothing to do with anyone else. You are, in and of yourself, a sexual being, meant to connect to yourself.

You might be thinking, "Am I supposed masturbate to connect to myself?" Even then, you are thinking about the act of orgasm as a means of connection. Instead, try and imagine yourself naked in front of a mirror. If you look at your body, you are only seeing half of yourself. Standing before you is a spirit as well. *Your* spirit. And this spirit is infinitely useful in understanding your own sexuality. If, looking at your naked self, you cannot feel your own spirit dwelling within you, then you are not connected to yourself. How, then, can you use sex to connect to anyone else? Our pursuit for connection to others through sexual acts like masturbation and intercourse ultimately is medicine for our inability to connect to ourselves.

Who am I vs. Who I Am

In order to begin healing, the pain we carry and the medicine we use to cope with that pain has to be confronted first. It is important we continue to reiterate this point. Then the need for the medicine can start to dissipate and you can see porn for what it is: a bunch of God's beautiful creations using theirs or other peoples' bodies to make money off of a bunch of hurting people.

You will also be able to more clearly see *what it isn't.*

It's not connection; it's division. It's a lot of things but it's not *sexual.* Because in that word is embedded a truth about the human spirit, and in porn, we find that truth missing.

So this brings us to a very important and misunderstood word: *identity.* I want to talk about who you were at the Beginning of Time. We're going to examine the You that resides in Perfection: the *You* without sin at all, not because Jesus "cleared the board," when he died and rose again as it were, but because the board never existed.

It is the true nature of Christ's sacrifice: *freedom* from sin in the most real sense. It is life as if sin and all the systems we attach to that word *did not exist.* And we experience it at first in glimpses as we heal and then later in larger pieces. I believe that not far down the road, we can live it as an everyday reality.

You have been given a body and when it was given to you, part of its purpose was to enjoy your sex drive. This is very important to understand, for while your desires might or might not be harmful to you right now, your desires are *not* your enemy; they are layers to be peeled back, one by one, letting the light of healing permeate each place. Your desires are your teacher, even the erotic ones.

Our most erotic desires are often where we hold our most shame. We like *this or that,* but we're often ashamed of it and we don't know why. It is in this feeling of shame where we can uncover the pain that is being medicated. This doesn't mean that if we heal, we'll all end up with nothing but the missionary position. But it does mean that joy will flood our desires. And shame and joy cannot occupy the same space. On the other side of shame, you may or may not want the same things sexually, but no matter what you want, you'll find joy and freedom in the experience.

Whether you are religious or not, take a moment and ask yourself, what does the Kingdom of God look like to you? How have you, with all your beliefs and imperfections, come to define what this kingdom that Jesus said is within you is or is not? Is it your hope that you will someday arrive at a place called Heaven and all your sinful desires will be magically taken away? Or is the Kingdom a place where sex doesn't exist at all? If not, why not? And does that make you happy? Or does it confuse you or make you angry?

When we ask these questions inside ourselves and answer them honestly, we can tune into what we truly feel and thus what we truly believe in our core. The Spirit of God, which can lead us into all truth, is not afraid of our honesty and vulnerability. It never has been.

Connecting to Yourself: A Simple Exercise

When I talk to my boys about God, they inevitably ask questions like "where is God?" and "can you talk to God?" I always try to teach them about prayer; one day my middle son (who is my Scottish redhead and the most sensitive of my boys) said, "Dad, how do I hear God?" It was a great question. In Christianity, we often put far too much emphasis on talking but very little on listening. And when we do talk about listening to God, we more often refer to something that resembles *decoding* with the purpose of trying to understand God's will.

Many Christians will also say that God speaks through scripture, but we know that reading scripture requires a lot of interpretation and understanding. The wisest among us study the Bible for years, read the original languages and then come to different conclusions about what it means. But if we teach our children that God listens to our prayers, then it would be logical that we would teach them that God speaks back through them as well. It would make sense that the spiritual channel is open on both ends.

So how do we listen to God? Sitting on my son's bed that night, I said, "So here's what I think: when we pray, we are talking to God. And meditation is listening to God." He said, "Oh, okay." Simple. And just as he had once asked, "How do you pray?" his next question was, of course, "How do you meditate?"

The word *meditation* can, at times but not always, cause problems for us in the Christian world. Some Christians have in-grown fears about Eastern religions and their approach to meditation. In many Eastern traditions, meditation is a silencing of the mind, with the ultimate goal of stillness in mind and body so that the spirit can lead. In much of traditional Christianity, meditation has had a more contemplative definition, calling to mind the 8th Century monk, quietly dwelling in the abbey, writing down thoughts rooted in scriptural study. For our purposes, I'd like to use the same definition I gave my son. And we're going to give it a shot because it's going to be helpful in the next chapter.

Below are four sentences I would like you to say. Pick a sentence and, when you're ready, sit down on the floor, take three deep breaths, close your eyes, and say your chosen sentence as you exhale. Say it three times slowly and intentionally. Observe how it makes you feel. Understand that by saying these things, you are doing nothing wrong, but if you feel guilt, shame, pain, or numbness anywhere (meaning that those feelings manifest in your body—perhaps a knot in the stomach or tightness in the chest or an inability to feel anything at all), then make a note of it.

Some of these statements might not be "true" as you understand it consciously, but try to say them anyway, because some of them may trigger emotions inside you that are important to pay attention to. Don't get hung up on whether you believe the sentence to be morally okay. You are two people, both conscious and unconscious, and this work is meant to create a greater connection between the two by awakening and empowering your spirit.

Here are the sentences:

1) My name is _____ and I am a sexual person.

2) My body has been given to me and I can do whatever I want with it without shame.

3) I find _____ to be erotic and attractive and that's okay.

4) This is my body. Every part of it is beautiful and sexy.

Now sit with those feelings and simply breathe for a while. Try not to let your mind race and cut you off from what you are feeling inside. Did the sentences make you uncomfortable? How do you feel? Right now, you might feel nothing. You might feel anger. You might be ready to explode in tears. You might want to find me and rip my head off. Whatever it is, keep your awareness there. Don't put the book down. Instead, read through the next chapter because however you feel, those feelings are important, and it is a marker on your path to finding the freedom you have been craving. In this final chapter, we are going to take everything we've learned and apply it.

For those of you who didn't try the meditation, that's okay. But I'd ask that you examine the reasons why you didn't want to try it. Was it fear? Loyalty to a belief? Time crunch? Be honest about it and then stay aware of those feelings. Essentially, being aware of those feelings is just as important as anything that you can dig up by way of meditation. And they will be just as useful in the next chapter.

By the way, it takes no small amount of courage to do all of this.

Read on.

chapter 10
DARING TO MOVE

In 2000, the band Switchfoot recorded a catchy song
called "Dare You to Move." The song is a literal dare, calling people to the present where forgiveness exists and
where the "Economy of Mercy" (same band, different song)
has more than enough grace for every one. But the real
thrust of the song, with its rock-ballad riffs pushing through
your core, is the central truth in this final chapter: none
of what you just learned matters for your life unless you
choose to *act*.

You have to move. You have to pick yourself up off of
the floor.

We're all familiar with this language and this struggle. In
our various states of depression, we tend to hate this idea
that we have *to do* something. We've all grunted and sweat
and tried to grind out some sort of hope or change—many

times with few or no results except more frustration or shame. So, what is the difference in this movement I speak of? It's in the paradigm shift. The difference is that the mystery of hope resides in this paradigm of our self and of God. We're not at war—so don't get ready for battle; we're on a pilgrimage—so be ready to take steps. There is hope in front of us, a light we can see if we have the courage to look. And this hope can lead us to a different type of action than before, one that sits squarely in the center of a Spirit-led quest into the unknown.

In one critical stanza of *Dare You To Move*, Jon Foreman (the songwriter) tells us:

> *Welcome to the fallout*
> *Welcome to resistance*
> *The tension is here*
> *Tension is here*
> *Between who you are and who you could be*
> *Between how it is and how it should be*

Inside of this fallout is the tension that illuminates the door to healing and transformation. The question is, *can you feel the tension?* Most of us cannot—we're too numb. This is why this issue is so strong in the Christian church and in the broader world. Being rid of slavery to porn addiction is part of this process, but my brother and I have experienced something far out beyond this sobriety that has to do with why we are here on this planet and the joy and peace and love we were meant to experience in this life.

That being said, in this final chapter, I am going to dare you to move. I am going to dare you to begin a Sacred Journey into the unknown with your heart set on finding freedom at all costs. And I am going to give you some tools for the journey.

The Main Thing

Earlier, we talked about meditation being a way to quiet the mind and stop all the noise that we deal with constantly. *Processing*, which we aim to teach here at a basic level, is meditation with a purpose other than simply growing quiet. Growing quiet is a wonderful aspect of meditation and allows us to open our ears and hearts to what the Spirit is saying to us. The problem with that comes when there is so much pain in the way that we are stuck in our heads and cannot truly be silent, because it is much harder than it sounds. The most common response I hear when someone tries meditation for the first time is usually something like, "I couldn't get my mind to stop." They can't keep from thinking. As soon as they attempt to be still, their mind races so hard that the idea of not thinking seems absurd. Some have referred to the mind as the "ego." Sounds about right. That's the part of us that is bent on control at all costs. And it stands in the way of us surrendering our pain to be healed.

Touchy-Feely

In Western culture, we idealize the mind. We seem to have an idea that the mind is who we are. We consider the mind the root of wisdom and even think that the voice we hear in our heads is *who we are.* We glorify education and the educated and we praise intelligence. Many people in our culture were raised with these ideals and, as a result of this, we not only have developed the ability to cut ourselves off from and suppress our spirits (which partner with our emotions), but we have also come to believe *unconsciously* that we can control our entire world with our intellects and belief systems.

All the control we give our minds disconnects us from a fundamental simple truth: We all know somewhere deep down that what we want—what we really want—is to *feel* okay. Or better still, *we want to feel amazing—an abundant life.* That's why one of the easy solutions is to pop some medication. You can take a pill that can reorganize your brain chemistry in a way that allows you to feel good while the medicine is in effect.

We've forgotten how to trust our feelings, especially us Christians. We're even degrading towards our feelings, especially in masculine culture, where we talk about the concept of feeling as something that lacks any type of truth. Those of us who emphasize feeling are often labeled as *touchy-feely* or *soft* in some way. And yet, here we are as a culture, collectively and desperately seeking something that will allow us to wake up and *feel* good about our lives.

Dave started to lead you into an exercise in the last chapter that is meant to quiet the mind and draw up the emotions. He used a phrase in the last chapter that is key here: *emotional truth.* For this to be helpful, we must accept that our emotions are the key to a deep truth, and that the body is the gateway to that truth. The reason you feel anxiety, fear, depression, and the numbness that accompanies addiction *in your body* is because your body is the vessel where we hold, remember, and experience *everything.* Our goal in turning your gaze from a religious truth that is external (of the mind), towards *The Kingdom of God that is within you* is to locate the pain in your body, which is made up of the inseparable elements of emo-tional and spiritual wounds inside of you. This is what you are medicating.

Now comes the practice part. When I first started this, my brother gave me a very simple meditation — just breathing and learning to feel instead of think. He told me to try it for ten minutes at a time (and longer if I could), so I did. I was desperate and was witnessing his transformation, so I just abandoned control and tried stuff.

What I experienced happened to me after about three or four attempts at meditation. Yes, it happened that fast. I had gone to see a therapist one time also, and we did some good inner examination in that session. But that's all I had done before this thing went down. I hadn't done any workshops in Alaska or gone on some quest in the desert. I had just spent a little bit of dedicated time in my closet and, most importantly, I had switched my paradigm. My intent had become passionately set on an inward journey instead of an outward process.

And in my story, that's when the experience of transformation took over – and it was radical. The twists and turns of your story may be different than mine, but like I did, you will experience the transformation you are seeking if you take what I am about to teach you and start making it a daily discipline. (There's that doing thing again.)

So, to begin, an exercise—I will give brief instructions with some stories and explanation for each. It will be helpful to read through this whole chapter and, once you understand each point, begin the exercise, utilizing what you have learned.

10 Minutes of Silence

This exercise is both very simple and very difficult at the same time:

1. *Find somewhere quiet and dark where you can sit or lay down.*
You need quiet and darkness because the mind tends to grab onto any stimulus very quickly and start heading some odd direction. It drives us from our bodies into our heads

instantly. It is the ever-present noise of our culture. Yes, I am saying technology does damage in this way. If you can't get somewhere dark, then cover your eyes with a blindfold of some sort, but silence is essential. Sometimes ambient sounds can help, but be careful to observe if your mind races somewhere else because of the sounds or if the sounds help you feel your internal self. When I first heard Dave's stories and tried to implement what he did, I used our bedroom closet, which was just big enough for me to lie down. At times, when trying to access my pain, my body would shut down and put me to sleep. If that happens to you, simply observe it without judgment. You probably need the rest anyway.

2. *Begin by breathing slowly. Fill your entire body with air.* The Bible, in its original languages, speaks of the *ruach* (in Hebrew) or the *pneuma* (in Greek) of God, which are words that mean both "breath" and "spirit" or "soul" of God. For instance, in the creation story in Genesis, when God created man, the text says God breathed the "breath of life" into man. "The Spirit of Life" is another way to understand this. For this reason, many cultures have understood that breathing is an important part of spiritual meditation and the experience of God.

Again, this isn't as easy as it sounds. As you begin to breathe, focus your attention on your breath. You will notice that your mind will try to jump in and start the race again.

When I first was on the floor in the closet, I could only get five or six breaths out before my mind would start racing and my breathing would get harder. As I relaxed my body, sometimes my chest would get heavy. This, as I understand it now, was the process of my body going into shutdown/protective mode. The breath has a way of opening up the body to *feel* what's inside; if you've inadvertently trained your body to keep pain and emotion suppressed, the defenses may come up very fast and try to shut down the breath.

Try to notice where you begin to identify with your thoughts and are unable to observe them. I remember (and sometimes still experience) my mind taking off in some crazy direction and it would be five minutes or so before I noticed I was thinking about the starting lineup for the next Sounders game.

It's okay, though. Just keep breathing—faster if you need to. This is where using some guided imagery in your mind can be helpful to focus the mind and allow some room for the body to step in and feel. That simply means that you imagine a narrative in your mind, perhaps recalling a time where you were triggered or imagining an interaction with that object or person that triggers your pain. Even imagining yourself hiking or running up a mountain can help create focus.

3. *Feel, don't think.*

For ten minutes, give your mind a vacation from running

your world. Your goal here is to breathe for ten minutes and feel what's in your body. We're not attempting to transform your whole universe or teleport you to Heaven and back. The goal is to go inward and simply feel. Observe what happens as you do this. Again, notice if your mind starts racing. Don't judge it as good or bad—that's simply unhelpful. If your mind begins racing, try to silence it again. If it helps, practice feeling sections of your body. It's especially helpful to feel the places where you most carry your stress. For instance, many people, myself included, experience a tremendous amount of their stress in their stomachs or in their chests. When my friend Pat gets triggered, he feels something painful in his middle-lower back. If you are able to feel these sensations (or any sensation including numbness which *feels* like the absence of feeling all together), you are already experiencing a deeper awareness of yourself.

I often ask people, "What are you feeling?" and their answer is something like "I'm feeling angry" or "I'm frustrated." Those are what we can call *secondary emotions*—they are the emotion over the top of the deeper emotion. This is very important because we could very easily stop with these emotions and attempt to control them, but these emotions are being generated from a wound underneath. For instance, anger may be how the true pain manifests, because most of us carry wounds that warrant real anger. But what is the actual reason we are angry? That is the true emotion underneath. In my case, I have discovered a great deal of pain from the experience of emotional abandonment within myself. Of course anger is generated from that experience, and for good reason. The anger might need to be moved or even experienced in order to be healed, but to do that, in meditation, we seek to feel the actual pain *in our bodies.*

4. *Pray—because God is with you.*

Remember that prayer is the act of talking to God, while meditation is the act of listening to God. Know this: God is with you. But in this step, I am not saying to take over the conversation. I am saying that as you do this process, it is possible that you will begin to feel things in your body. You might feel something you are familiar with but perhaps had never focused on before. A prayer that can be helpful here is something very simple such as: place your hand over the area in your body that you are feeling the pain/discomfort/familiar weirdness and say something like, "Show me what this is." That simple. There are very few words required in our prayer when our intent is on allowing the Spirit to move inside of us. But, for reasons I can't say I fully understand, I believe speaking things aloud is important. Perhaps it's because one of the things that we learned to suppress inside of us is our voice. We struggle to *speak the truth we feel* and must therefore learn to speak again, just like we have to learn to feel again. God is with you, whether you know it or not and your prayer is heard and understood.

5. *Find Your Emotional Truth*

When I first began this process of allowing the Spirit to heal me and awaken my dormant spirit inside of my body, I discovered that there was some "truth" inside of me that was tough to categorize. Dave used the term "emotional truth" in the last chapter. I think that is helpful. We're not talking about *fact*. We're talking about *truth*.

For example, I give you Jesus on the cross: "Eloi! Eloi! Lama Sabacthani!" or translated from Aramaic, "My God! My God! Why have you abandoned me?!" This is traditionally called The Cry of Dereliction, and theologians for centuries have been arguing over whether God actually abandoned Jesus there on the cross or not. Was Jesus speaking from the depth of the human experience of abandonment or was he claiming something factual about God?

In my reading, I have come to see Jesus as fully uniting with the human experience right there on a Roman execution stake. I have come to read the crucifixion of Jesus this way because it seems to me that the core of the human experience is one of abandonment. Perhaps this is why we carry a seemingly uncontrollable and collective anxiety as a human race. This is the experience of crucifixion and we all hope for resurrection. But as Peter Rollins writes in *Insurrection,* if we want to experience that resurrection, we have to go through the crucifixion first rather than suppress it down inside of ourselves. In the Cry of Dereliction, Jesus is expressing a deep *emotional and spiritual truth* even though God might be understood theologically as ever present, right there with him on the cross.

So remember that as we pray in this process, there in the closet or on your bed or in your car or wherever you are, we must be able to be honest emotionally about what we're experiencing. Know that God is not afraid of your pain or doubt or anger. Jesus understood this deeply and screamed it out from his core. In fact, throughout the Hebrew Scriptures, we see a tradition of people blasting God with what their agony and experience. This cannot be ignored. God sees us. So keep breathing and be honest. God hears you. So feel that pain and observe it. And withhold judgment of yourself.

6. *Be prepared to let some things out.*
As you learn to breathe, feel, and pray truthfully, your spirit will be activated. You're asking your spirit and the Spirit of God to begin to heal you. You might struggle to feel anything at first, but if you keep working in this way, it's simply a matter of time until it begins. If you feel nothing, understand that feeling nothing is still feeling something, but, when the time comes that you feel *that thing* you have always felt but never really felt—that thing that you have been medicating for so long, your spirit is going to start to try to kick it out of your body.

For me, it started with coughing. The more intensely I

would feel those butterflies, the more I would cough. Sometimes I would yawn. I even threw up. Sometimes, I would want to scream, so I grabbed a pillow, put my face into it, and let it out. And I spent a great deal of time weeping because so much of the pain that was trapped inside of my body was really a mountain of grief.

I found that afterward, I often felt very different, like some part of me had moved out and been replaced with something far better. Sometimes I would feel peace. Sometimes I would feel like I had just disturbed a hornets' nest and there was a great deal more work to do.

If this is what you experience, it is very important to continue working, though perhaps not that day. Your pain will continue to resist being removed. Don't stop—dare yourself to move time and time again. No matter what I experienced, every time I would do this, I would learn something. A great deal of this learning revolved around my ability to hear the voice of the Spirit of God and decide that, as it led me into the unknown, I could trust that voice. This is the place where all of my belief became something that placed boots on the road. This is where my pilgrimage grew legs and began to walk.

The Process in Brief

So, to review the basics of processing:

1. *Find somewhere quiet and dark where you can sit or lay down.*
2. *Begin by breathing slowly. Fill your entire body with air.*

3. *Feel, don't think.*
4. *Pray—because God is with you.*
5. *Find your emotional truth.*
6. *Be prepared to let some things out.*

You can take as much time as you want, but I would say that your minimum goal should be ten minutes of processing to begin with. You can certainly do it for less time, but in my experience, it takes at least five minutes or so before I start to feel the resistance that comes along with actual spiritual practice. When I can come to that place and stay engaged there for even another five minutes, I begin to experience things and learn a new way of being.

Your experience may be similar to mine, or it might not. These experiences can look very different for everyone, but they will move you forward, and as you do so, you can take more time, gaining wisdom as you start to have experiences that change you. The importance is doing this on a regular basis, daily if you can. Ten minutes should be doable daily for just about everyone and as you do this, you can begin to couple it with other types of therapy that present themselves to you as helpful. But you will always be moving forward.

This is what I did at the beginning and I started to see results very quickly, and I now have made processing a regular part of my life. My two children (under the age of two) have begun to exert more influence on the rhythms of my spiritual disciplines in recent times, but that's life. The key is that I have kept moving, and my life has become an infinitely happier existence. I have experienced miracles and my life continues to change more and more. The disciplines have changed for me as well. I meditate on a regular basis now for varying amounts of time and in different ways. Even my common experiences have become more meditative for me, like writing and playing soccer.

This is The Pilgrimage

This is "the work." I call it that because that's exactly what it is. It is the activation of tools you have been given by God to find healing in ways you might not have imagined were possible, and it begins with something this simple and yet this complex. Remember that as you do this, your pain will resist the process—it will demand medication until it is moved. Your ego will try to keep things repressed. Your mind will try to race and control things. Your body might try to shut down. All of these things can happen because that is what your body has been trained to do. You probably just have never known this.

And if you experience these types of resistance, remember that it's okay. Try not to judge it as good or bad, even if you give in and medicate your pain. Judging yourself again because you "fell off the horse" or "acted out" or "slipped up" is worthless. It isn't helpful, unless you can take a step back and observe that experience of feeling guilty and name it for what it is—pain attempting to medicate itself on self-hate. If you feel shame, feel the feeling instead of thinking the thoughts. The key is feeling the shame that resides as pain in your body. So take a deep breath. Baby steps are still steps and the Spirit of God, along with your spirit working hand in hand, will lead you. *Remember that feeling nothing is still feeling something.* The key to it is that train yourself to *feel* that nothingness. The path to freedom lies inside of that feeling.

I believe this because I have come to discover the most amazing thing about this journey: God actually exists and that the Spirit is real. I believe we have nothing to fear because our spirits possess all authority to heal us and give us freedom. I believe this not because I have been told to believe this or because if I don't there will be eternal consequences, but because I have experienced the truth of it. I had suffered to the point where I was willing to go somewhere new in order to determine what I believe Jesus was getting at when he spoke of experiencing an abundant life. I believe that what God wanted for me most wasn't religious devotion, but rather it was a peace that passes my understanding—which I believe is the hallmark of The Kingdom of God that is among us and within us.

One of the beautiful, but possibly disorienting side effects of this experience is that you begin to live in mystery. You can see clearly the wisdom you have acquired as you've walked the path of this pilgrimage, but as you look forward, there is always something to discover on that next horizon, over that next mountain. Concrete judgments and condemnations of things and people that lie outside of your understanding become more difficult to make. This is because the mystery of God dwells inside every human being, and every story that surrounds you every waking second of life. The more you learn, the less you know. And this is a wonderful experience.

Before we conclude this introduction to a new way of being, I want to be clear that what we have given you here is indeed a *beginning*. Should you choose to try this method, and if your experience is anything like mine, then as you move forward, you will experience pain and peace, hell and hope—but you will no longer be an addict. These things are all along the path of this pilgrimage and it will get easier, because each time the sun sets over that mountain in front of you, the Spirit will reassure you that the path you have chosen leads to life. As the questions come up, know that the Spirit will lead you. God knows what you need and can be trusted. Seek out help with this. Go to meetings, try different types of therapy—head up to Alaska and hang out with Floyd if you want. Read other books too, read this one again, sit with friends, and share your story and questions. Gauge the truth of these various things, including the things we have written and produced, based on whether it is *helpful or not.*

The point is—*move.* Try things. Seek freedom by any means necessary.

You are in the hands of the Spirit of God that still hovers over the deep. Sometimes you may encounter people who are afraid of your quest for healing. That's part of this journey. Some people will understand and some will not. Some see any quest into the unknown as dangerous; that type of resistance is the nature of the journey and Jesus said as much. He said that those who followed the path he was teaching would be hated by the world. I don't believe He meant "people who weren't Christians." He was talking about a world that would rather stand where they are and control things than walk into the unknown for the sake of losing their lives so that they could find them. And this includes the religious and non-religious alike—just like the path of truth- and life-seekers is made up of people from every walk.

This issue of porn addiction in the church is creating more and more seekers by the day, people who are willing to lose it all for the sake of love and a peace that passes their understanding.

And that's because our spirits are coming alive with power and authority, even in the darkness.

And that makes this experience of our sexuality a Sacred Journey, not a war.

See you on the road.

A NOTE ON THERAPY

I felt it necessary to write something brief about the kinds of therapy I see as helpful for those of us diving into this deep work in the area of unconscious or repressed pain. There are many modalities of therapy that can be helpful in a variety of ways. The most helpful ones, I have come to believe, are the ones that allow and facilitate an exploration into *feeling* (especially repressed emotion) as a way of healing. Some examples (but not all) of this are Lifespan Integration Therapy, Eye Movement Desensitization and Reprocessing (EMDR), Core Emotional Clearing or Rapid Transformational Therapy (what Dave found in Alaska), expressive therapies like Sandtray and Art Therapy, and Psychodynamic Attachment Based Therapy.

Coupling a lifestyle of simple meditative processing, like that taught in this book, spiritual paradigm shifts (external to internal), and these types of therapies can bring about dramatic change rapidly. That's because all of these things are helpful in awakening the spirit that has been suppressed along with the emotions. Your spirit is the key. It is connected to God and healing begins there. Blessings.

—Seth Taylor, October, 2014
Seattle, WA

ACKNOWLEDGEMENTS

It was almost two years ago that my brother called me and said, "It's time." Of course I asked what it was time to do. "Time to write," he said. We knew we had something to say and at the time, we planned on coauthoring this book but after awhile, it became clear that this project was mine to undertake with Dave contributing his stories and thoughts where needed. That being said, there is no one who deserves more credit for this book's existence than my brother David. He was the Gandalf to my Frodo.

Others that I place gratefully in the, without you, this never happens, category:

Amy—for far more reasons than I can ever write on a page.

Rob Bell—who gave me the "priestly blessing" of being willing to see my passion and teach me how to write a book.

Pete Rollins—Pete's work has impacted me and my thinking more than any writer I have ever encountered and you will most likely experience that in reading this book. I'm incredibly grateful for his willingness to sit with me, encourage me, and teach me to see in new ways.

John Phillip Newell—who was willing to hear my zillions of questions on Iona as I followed him like a lost dog and bless them as sacred.

Craig Gross—His vision and courage is the reason this book exists as it does, as well as the *Guidebook* and the other materials around it.

Mom and Dad Jones—Their support was the lifeline that kept the blood of this project pumping.

There are many others who deserve thanks and I wish I could list them all, but I also want to publicly thank: Adam Palmer (Mountain Man and Editing Wizard), Sam Vert (my Go-To-Guy), Theo Bremer-Bennett (design genie at Glyph Engine—still the coolest name for a design firm I've ever heard), Ryan Kuja (for wandering and wondering with me), my sister Rachel, Emily Davis, James Passey, Patrick Ianni, Kyle Dehnert, and Dan Redwine—for awesome conversations that shaped my thinking and for keeping us afloat when the "tornado(s)" hit. And thanks to Tyson for incredibly well-timed beers and being the friend that every man needs.

Finally, I want to thank the students, faculty, and staff of The Seattle School of Theology and Psychology. As Rob once said, that place is a "veritable hotbed of theological awesomeness disguised as a graduate school." It's also a sacred place of deep healing and I am grateful for every painful and powerful second I spent there.

Lacking a present time connection to grace of God, 1) Episc. seek comfort in repeating the Salvation story @ Sunday. + construct Evans reinforce ordo salutis wr/unwritten practices + giving them the mask pain + certs of hard to believe of...

God works by applying the (most fabricated) worldly goodness, of surr. society or the part we want the wells done, good + ... progressive from...

9/23/16

Made in the USA
San Bernardino, CA
06 May 2016

e. e. cummings

*was born in Cambridge, Massachusetts, in
1894. He attended Harvard where his father
had been an assistant professor of English.
In World War I, he went to France as an
ambulance driver and later served as a private in the American Army. It was during
his French experience that he wrote*
The Enormous Room *and with it achieved
a measure of popularity.*

*After the war he studied art in Paris. In
1925 he won the* Dial *prize and, in 1928, his
play,* him, *was produced by the Province-
town Players. Since then Cummings has
produced a steady flow of poetry and paintings. He is a member of the National In-
stitute of Arts and Letters, and in 1955 he
received a special citation from the National Book Awards committee for his*
Poems, 1923-1954.

*Cummings has written this about his
poetry: "So far as I am concerned, poetry
and every other art was and is and forever
will be strictly and distinctly a question of
individuality. . . . If poetry is your goal,
you've got to forget all about punishments
and all about rewards and all about self-
styled obligations and duties and responsi-
bilities etcetera ad infinitum and remember
one thing only: that it's you — nobody else
— who determine your destiny and decide
your fate."*

50

POEMS

E. E. Cummings

The Universal Library

GROSSET & DUNLAP

NEW YORK

to m. m.

Some of the poems in this book have appeared in *Furioso*, *Poetry*, and *Poetry Weekly*. Grateful acknowledgment is made for permission to reprint them.

INDEX OF FIRST LINES

POEMS

!blac
k
agains
t

(whi)

te sky
?t
rees whic
h fr

om droppe

d

,
le
af

a:;go

e
s wh
IrlI
n

·g

2

fl

a
tt
ene

d d

reaml
essn
esse

s wa

it
sp
i

t)(t

he
s
e

f

ooli
sh sh
apes

ccocoucougcoughcoughi

ng with me
n more o
n than in the

m

3

If you can't eat you got to

smoke and we aint got
nothing to smoke:come on kid

let's go to sleep
if you can't smoke you got to

Sing and we aint got

nothing to sing;come on kid
let's go to sleep

if you can't sing you got to
die and we aint got

Nothing to die,come on kid

let's go to sleep
if you can't die you got to

dream and we aint got
nothing to dream(come on kid

Let's go to sleep)

nobody loved **this**
he)with its
of eye stuck
into a rock of

forehead.No
body

loved
big that quick
sharp
thick snake of **a**

voice these

root
like legs
or
feethands;

nobody
ever could ever

had love loved whose **his**
climbing shoulders queerly **twilight**
:never,no
(body.

Nothing

am was. are leaves few this. is these a or
scratchily over which of earth dragged once
-ful leaf. & were who skies clutch an of poor
how colding hereless. air theres what immense
live without every dancing. singless only a child's eyes float silently down
more than two those that and that noing our
gone snow gone
                        yours mine
                                    . We're
alive and shall be:cities may overflow(am
was)assassinating whole grassblades,five
ideas can swallow a man;three words im
-prison a woman for all her now:but we've
such freedom such intense digestion so
much greenness only dying makes us grow

6

flotsam and jetsam
are gentlemen poeds
urseappeal netsam
our spinsters and coeds)

thoroughly bretish
they scout the inhuman
itarian fetish
that man isn't wuman

vive the millenni
um three cheers for labor
give all things to enni
one bugger thy nabor

(neck and senecktie
are gentlemen ppoyds
even whose recktie
are covered by lloyd's

7

moan
(is)
ing

the she of the
sea
un

der a who
a he a moon a
magic out

of the black this which of
one street leaps quick
squirmthicklying iu

minous night
mare som
e w

hereanynoevery
ing(danc)ing
wills&weres

8

the Noster was a ship of swank
(as gallant as they come)
until she hit a mine and sank
just off the coast of Sum

precisely where a craft of cost
the Ergo perished later
all hands(you may recall)being lost
including captain Pater

9

warped this perhapsy
stumbl
i
NgflounderpirouettiN
                        g

:seized(

tatterdemalion
dow
      nupfloatsw
                  oon
InG

s ly)tuck.s its(ghostsoul sheshape)

elf into leasting forever most
magical maybes of certainly
never the iswas

teetertiptotterish

sp-
    inwhirlpin
                  -wh
EEling
;a!who,

(

whic hbubble ssomethin
gabou tlov
e)

spoke joe to jack

leave her alone
she's not your gal

jack spoke to joe
's left crashed
pal dropped

o god alice
yells but who shot
up grabbing had
by my throat me

give it him good
a bottle she
quick who stop damned
fall all we go spill

and chairs tables the and
bitch whispers jill
mopping too bad

dear sh not yet
jesus what blood

darling i said

red-rag and pink-flag
blackshirt and brown
strut-mince and stink-brag
have all come to town

some like it shot
and some like it hung
and some like it in the two
nine months young

(will you teach a
wretch to live
straighter than a needle)

ask
    her
        ask
            when
                (ask **and**
                ask
                and ask

again and)ask a
brittle little
person fiddling
in
the
rain

(did you kiss
a girl with nipples
like pink thimbles)

ask
    him
        ask
            who
                (ask **and**
                ask
                and ask

ago and)ask a
simple
crazy
thing
singing
in the snow

proud of his scientific attitude

and liked the prince of wales wife wants to die
but the doctors won't let her comma considers frood
whom he pronounces young mistaken and
cradles in rubbery one somewhat hand
the paper destinies of nations sic
item a bounceless period unshy
the empty house is full O Yes of guk
rooms daughter item son a woopsing queer
colon hobby photography never has plumbed
the heights of prowst but respects artists if
they are sincere proud of his scientif
ic attitude and liked the king of)hear

ye!the godless are the dull and the dull are the damned

14

the way to hump a cow is not
to get yourself a stool
but draw a line around the spot
and call it beautifool

to multiply because and why
dividing thens by nows
and adding and(i understand)
is hows to hump a cows

the way to hump a cow is not
to elevate your tool
but drop a penny in the slot
and bellow like a bool

to lay a wreath from ancient greath
on insulated brows
(while tossing boms at uncle toms)
is hows to hump a cows

the way to hump a cow is not
to push and then to pull
but practicing the art of swot
to preach the golden rull

to vote for me(all decent mem
and wonens will allows
which if they don't to hell with them)
is hows to hump a cows

15

mrs

& mr across the way are kind of
afraid)afraid

of what(of

a crazy man)don't
ask me how i know(a he of head
comes to some dirty window every)twilight i

feel(his lousy eyes roaming)wonderful all

sky(a little mouth)stumbling(can't
keep up with how big very
them)now(it tears
off rag its

of

mind chucks away flimsy
which but)always(they're
more much further off)further these
those three disappear finally what's left

behind is(just a head of he

is)merely(a pair of ears with some
lips plus a couple of)holes probably that's what
(mr & mrs are

sort of really

really kind
of afraid of)these(down pull & who'll

shades

)when what hugs stopping earth than silent is
more silent than more than much more is or
total sun oceaning than any this
tear jumping from each most least eye of star

and without was if minus and shall be
immeasurable happenless unnow
shuts more than open could that every tree
or than all life more death begins to grow

end's ending then these dolls of joy and grief
these recent memories of future dream
these perhaps who have lost their shadows if
which did not do the losing spectres mime

until out of merely not nothing comes
only one snowflake(and we speak our names

youful

larger
of smallish)

Humble a
rosily
,nimblest;

c-urlin-g
noworld
Silent is

blue
(sleep!new

girlgold

18

ecco a letter starting "dearest we"
unsigned:remarkably brief but covering
one complete miracle of nearest far

"i cordially invite me to become
noone except yourselves r s v p"

she cannot read or write,la moon. Employs
a very crazily how clownlike that
this quickly ghost scribbling from there to where

—name unless i'm mistaken chauvesouris—
whose grammar is atrocious;but so what

princess selene doesn't know a thing
who's much too busy being her beautiful yes.
The place is now
                    let us accept
                            (the time

forever,and you'll wear your silver shoes

19

there is a here and

that here was a
town(and the town is

so aged the ocean
wanders the streets are so
ancient the houses enter the

people are so feeble the feeble go to
sleep if the people sit down)
and this light is so dark the mountains
grow up from

the sky is so near the earth does not
open her
eyes(but the
feeble are people the feeble
are so wise the people

remember being born)
when and
if nothing disappears they
will disappear always who are filled

with never are more than
more is are mostly
almost are feebler than feeble are

fable who are less than these are least is who
are am(beyond when behind where under

un)

harder perhaps than a newengland bed

these ends of arms which pinch that purple book
between what hands had been before they died

squirming:now withered and unself her gnarled
vomits a rock of mindscream into life;
possibly darker than a spinster's heart

my voice feels who inquires is your cough
better today?nn-nn went head face goes

(if how begins a pillow's green means face

or why a quilt's pink stops might equal head).
Then with the splendor of an angel's fart

came one trembling out of huge each eye look
"thank you" nicely the lady's small grin said
(with more simplicity than makes a world)

six

are in a room's dark around)
five

(are all dancesing singdance all are

three
with faces made of cloud dancing and
three
singing with voices made of earth and

six are in a room's dark around)

five
(six are in a room's)
one

is red

and(six are in)
four are

white

(three singdance six dancesing three
all around around all
clouds singing three and
and three dancing earths

three menandwomen three

and all around all and
all around five all
around five around)

five flowers five

(six are in a room's dark)
all five are one

flowers five flowers and all one is fire

nouns to nouns

wan
wan

too nons two

and
and

nuns two nuns

w an d
ering

in sin

g
ular untheknowndulous s

pring

a pretty a day
(and every fades)
is here and away
(but born are maids
to flower an hour
in all,all)

o yes to flower
until so blithe
a doer a wooer
some limber and lithe
some very fine mower
a tall;tall

some jerry so very
(and nellie and fan)
some handsomest harry
(and sally and nan
they tremble and cower
so pale:pale)

for betty was born
to never say nay
but lucy could learn
and lily could pray
and fewer were shyer
than doll. doll

these people socalled were not given hearts
how should they be?their socalled hearts would **think**
these socalled people have no minds but if
they had their minds socalled would not exist

but if these not existing minds took life
such life could not begin to live id est
breathe but if such life could its breath would **stink**

and as for souls why souls are wholes not parts
but all these hundreds upon thousands of
people socalled if multiplied by twice
infinity could never equal one)

which may your million selves and my suffice
to through the only mystery of love
become while every sun goes round its moon

25

as freedom is a breakfastfood
or truth can live with right and wrong
or molehills are from mountains made
—long enough and just so long
will being pay the rent of seem
and genius please the talentgang
and water most encourage flame

as hatracks into peachtrees grow
or hopes dance best on bald men's hair
and every finger is a toe
and any courage is a fear
—long enough and just so long
will the impure think all things pure
and hornets wail by children stung

or as the seeing are the blind
and robins never welcome spring
nor flatfolk prove their world is round
nor dingsters die at break of dong
and common's rare and millstones float
—long enough and just so long
tomorrow will not be too late

worms are the words but joy's the voice
down shall go which and up come who
breasts will be breasts thighs will be thighs
deeds cannot dream what dreams can do
—time is a tree(this life one leaf)
but love is the sky and i am for you
just so long and long enough

wherelings whenlings
(daughters of ifbut offspring of hopefear
sons of unless and children of almost)
never shall guess the dimension of

him whose
each
foot likes the
here of this earth

whose both
eyes
love
this now of the sky

—endlings of isn't
shall never
begin
to begin to

imagine how(only are shall be were
dawn dark rain snow rain
-bow &
a

moon
's whis-
per
in sunset

or thrushes toward dusk among whippoorwills **or**
tree field rock hollyhock forest brook chickadee
mountain. Mountain)
whycoloured worlds of because do

not stand against yes which is built by
forever & sunsmell
(sometimes a wonder
of wild roses

sometimes)
with north
over
the barn

27

buy me an ounce and i'll sell you a pound.
Turn
gert
        (spin!
helen)the
slimmer the finger the thicker the thumb(it's
whirl,
girls)
round and round

early to better is wiser for worse.
Give
liz
        (take!
tommy)we
order a steak and they send us a pie(it's
try,
boys)
mine is yours

ask me the name of the moon in the man.
Up
sam
        (down!
alice)a
hole in the ocean will never be missed(it's
in,
girls)
yours is mine

either was deafer than neither was dumb.
Skip
fred
        (jump!
neddy)but
under the wonder is over the why(it's
now,
boys)
here we come

28

there are possibly 2½ or impossibly 3
individuals every several fat
thousand years. Expecting more would be
neither fantastic nor pathological but

dumb. The number of times a wheel turns
doesn't determine its roundness:if swallows tryst
in your barn be glad;nobody ever earns
anything,everything little looks big in a mist

and if(by Him Whose blood was for us spilled)
than all mankind something more small occurs
or something more distorting than socalled
civilization i'll kiss a stalinist arse

in hitler's window on wednesday next at 1
E.S.T. bring the kiddies let's all have fun

anyone lived in a pretty how town
(with up so floating many bells down)
spring summer autumn winter
he sang his didn't he danced his dia.

Women and men(both little and small)
cared ror anyone not at all
they sowed their isn't they reaped their same
sun moon stars rain

children guessed(but only a few
and down they forgot as up they grew
autumn winter spring summer)
that noone loved him more by more

when by now and tree by leaf
she laughed his joy she cried his grief
bird by snow and stir by still
anyone's any was all to her

someones married their everyones
laughed their cryings and did their dance
(sleep wake hope and then)they
said their nevers they slept their dream

stars rain sun moon
(and only the snow can begin to explain
how children are apt to forget to remember
with up so floating many bells down)

one day anyone died i guess
(and noone stooped to kiss his face)
busy folk buried them side by side
little by little and was by was

all by all and deep by deep
and more by more they dream their sleep
noone and anyone earth by april
wish by spirit and if by yes.

Women and men(both dong and ding)
summer autumn winter spring
reaped their sowing and went their came
sun moon stars rain

the silently little blue elephant shyly(he was terri
bly
warped by his voyage from every to no)who
still stands still as found some lost thing(like a
curtain on which tiny the was painted in round
blue but quite now it's swirly and foldish so only through)the
little blue elephant at the zoo(jumbled
to queer this what that a here and
there a peers at you)has(elephant the blue)put some just
a now and now little the(on his quiet
head his magical shoulders him doll
self)hay completely thus or that wispily
is to say according to his perfect
satisfaction vanishing from a this world into bigger
much some out of(not visible to us)whom only his dream
ing own soul looks
and
the is all floatful and remembering

31

not time's how(anchored in what mountaining *r*oots
of mere eternity)stupendous if
discoverably disappearing floats
at trillionworlded the ecstatic ease

with which vast my complexly wisdoming friend's
—a fingery treesoul onlying from serene
whom queries not suspected selves of space—
life stands gradually upon four minds

(out of some undering joy and overing grief
nothing arrives a so prodigious am
a so immediate is escorts us home
through never's always until absolute un

gulps the first knowledge of death's wandering guess)
while children climb their eyes to touch his dream

newlys of silence
(both an only

moon the with star

one moving are twilight
they beyond near)

girlest she slender

is cradling in joy her
flower than now

(softlying wisdoms

enter guess)
childmoon smile to

your breathing doll

one slipslouch twi
tterstamp
coon wid a plon
kykerplung
guit
ar
   (pleez make me glad)dis

dumdam slamslum slopp
idy wurl
sho am
wick
id id
ar
   (now heer we kum dearie)bud

hooz
gwine ter
hate
dad hurt
fool wurl no gal no
boy
    (day simbully loves id)fer

ids dare
pain dares un
no
budy elses un ids
dare dare
joy
   (eye kinely thank yoo)

my father moved through dooms of love
through sames of am through haves of give,
singing each morning out of each night
my father moved through depths of height

this motionless forgetful where
turned at his glance to shining here;
that if(so timid air is firm)
under his eyes would stir and squirm

newly as from unburied which
floats the first who,his april touch
drove sleeping selves to swarm their fates
woke dreamers to their ghostly roots

and should some why completely weep
my father's fingers brought her sleep:
vainly no smallest voice might cry
for he could feel the mountains grow.

Lifting the valleys of the sea
my father moved through griefs of joy;
praising a forehead called the moon
singing desire into begin

joy was his song and joy so pure
a heart of star by him could steer
and pure so now and now so yes
the wrists of twilight would rejoice

keen as midsummer's keen beyond
conceiving mind of sun will stand,
so strictly(over utmost him
so hugely)stood my father's dream

his flesh was flesh his blood was blood:
no hungry man but wished him food;
no cripple wouldn't creep one mile
uphill to only see him smile.

Scorning the pomp of must and shall
my father moved through dooms of feel;

his anger was as right as rain
his pity was as green as grain

septembering arms of year extend
less humbly wealth to foe and friend
than he to foolish and to wise
offered immeasurable is

proudly and(by octobering flame
beckoned)as earth will downward climb,
so naked for immortal work
his shoulders marched against the dark

his sorrow was as true as bread:
no liar looked him in the head;
if every friend became his foe
he'd laugh and build a world with snow.

My father moved through theys of we,
singing each new leaf out of each tree
(and every child was sure that spring
danced when she heard my father sing)

then let men kill which cannot share,
let blood and flesh be mud and mire,
scheming imagine,passion willed,
freedom a drug that's bought and sold

giving to steal and cruel kind,
a heart to fear,to doubt a mind,
to differ a disease of same,
conform the pinnacle of am

though dull were all we taste as bright,
bitter all utterly things sweet,
maggoty minus and dumb death
all we inherit,all bequeath

and nothing quite so least as truth
—i say though hate were why men breathe—
because my father lived his soul
love is the whole and more than all

you which could grin three smiles into a dead
house clutch between eyes emptiness toss one

at nobody shoulder and thick stickingly un

stride after glide massacre monday did
more)ask a lifelump buried by the star
nicked ends next among broken odds of yes
terday's tomorrow(than today can guess

or fears to dare whatever dares to fear)

i very humbly thank you which could grin
may stern particular Love surround your trite
how terrible selfhood with its hands and feet

(lift and may pitying Who from sharp soft worms

of spiralling why and out of black because
your absolute courage with its legs and arms

i say no world

can hold a you
shall see the not
because
and why but
(who
stood within his steam beginning and
began to sing all
here is hands machine no

good too quick i know this
suit you pay
a store too
much yes what
too much o much cheap
me i work i know i say i have
not any
never
no vacation here

is hands is work since i am
born is good
but there this cheap this suit too
quick no suit there every
-thing
nothing i
say the
world not fit
you)he is

not(i say the world
yes any world is much
too not quite big enough to
hold one tiny this with
time's
more than
most how
immeasurable
anguish

pregnant one fearless
one good yes
completely kind
mindheart one true one generous child-
man
-god one eager
souldoll one
unsellable not buyable alive
one i say human being)one

goldberger

37

these children singing in stone a
silence of stone these
little children wound with stone
flowers opening for

ever these silently lit
tle children are petals
their song is a flower of
always their flowers

of stone are
silently singing
a song more silent
than silence these always

children forever
singing wreathed with singing
blossoms children of
stone with blossoming

eyes
know if a
lit tle
tree listens

forever to always children singing forever
a song made
of silent as stone silence of
song

love is the every only god

who spoke this earth so glad and big
even a thing all small and sad
man,may his mighty briefness dig

for love beginning means return
seas who could sing so deep and strong

one queerying wave will whitely yearn
from each last shore and home come young

so truly perfectly the skies
by merciful love whispered were,
completes its brightness with your eyes

any illimitable star

denied night's face
have shadowless they?
i bring you peace
the moon of day

predicted end
who never began
of god and fiend?
i give you man

extracted hate
from whispering grass?
joy in time shut
and starved on space?

love's murdered eye
dissected to mere
because and why?
take this whole tear.

By handless hints
do conjurers rule?
do mannikins
forbid the soul?

is death a whore
with life's disease
which quacks will cure
when pimps may please?

must through unstrange
synthetic now
true histories plunge?
rains a grey snow

of mothery same
rotting keen dream?
i rise which am
the sun of whom

a peopleshaped toomany-ness far **too**

and will it tell us who we are and will
it tell us why we dream and will it tell
us how we drink crawl eat walk die fly do?

a notalive undead too-nearishness

and shall we cry and shall we laugh and shall
entirely our doom steer his great small
wish into upward deepness of less fear
much than more climbing hope meets most despair?

all knowing's having and have is(you guess)
perhaps the very unkindest way to kill
each of those creatures called one's self so **we'll**

not have(but i imagine that yes is
the only living thing)and we'll make **yes**

up into the silence the green
silence with a white earth in it

you will(kiss me)go

out into the morning the young
morning with a warm world in it

(kiss me)you will go

on into the sunlight the fine
sunlight with a firm day in it

you will go(kiss me

down into your memory and
a memory and memory

i)kiss me(will go)

love is more thicker than forget
more thinner than recall
more seldom than a wave is wet
more frequent than to fail

it is most mad and moonly
and less it shall unbe
than all the sea which only
is deeper than the sea

love is less always than to win
less never than alive
less bigger than the least begin
less littler than forgive

it is most sane and sunly
and more it cannot die
than all the sky which only
is higher than the sky

hate blows a bubble of despair into
hugeness world system universe and bang
—fear buries a tomorrow under woe
and up comes yesterday most green and young

pleasure and pain are merely surfaces
(one itself showing,itself hiding one)
life's only and true value neither is
love makes the little thickness of the coin

comes here a man would have from madame death
neverless now and without winter spring?
she'll spin that spirit her own fingers with
and give him nothing(if he should not sing)

how much more than enough for both of us
darling. And if i sing you are my voice,

air,

be
comes
or

 (a)

   new
   (live)
   now

    ;&

     th
     (is no littler
     th

   an a:

   fear no bigger
   th
   an a

  hope)is

st
anding
st

a.r

45

enters give
whose lost is his found
leading love
whose heart is her mind)

supremely whole
uplifting the,
of each where all
was is to be

welcomes welcomes
her dreams his face
(her face his dreams
rejoice rejoice)

—opens the sun:
who music wear
burst icy known
swim ignorant fire

(adventuring
and time's dead which;
falling falling
both locked in each

down a thief by
a whore dragged goes
to meet her why
she his because

46

grEEn's d

an
cing on hollow was

young Up
floatingly clothes tumbledish
olD(with

sprouts o
ver and)a-
live
wanders remembe

r
ing per
F
ectl
y

crumb
ling eye
-holes oUt of whe
reful whom(leas

tly)
smiles the
infinite nothing

of
M

an

(sitting in a tree-)
o small you
sitting in a tree-

sitting in a treetop

riding on a greenest

riding on a greener
(o little i)
riding on a leaf

o least who
sing small thing
dance little joy

(shine most prayer)

mortals)

climbi
        ng i
        nto eachness begi
        n
dizzily
        swingthings
of speeds of
trapeze gush somersaults
open ing
            hes shes
&meet&
        swoop
            fully is are ex
                        quisite theys of re
turn
        a
        n
        d
fall which now drop who all dreamlike

(im

i am so glad and very
merely my fourth will cure
the laziest self of weary
the hugest sea of shore

so far your nearness reaches
a lucky fifth of you
turns people into eachs
and cowards into grow

our can'ts were born to happen
our mosts have died in more
our twentieth will open
wide a wide open door

we are so both and oneful
night cannot be so sky
sky cannot be so sunful
i am through you so i

what freedom's not some under's mere above
but breathing yes which fear will never no?
measureless our pure living complete love
whose doom is beauty and its fate to grow

shall hate confound the wise?doubt blind the brave?
does mask wear face?have singings gone to say?
here youngest selves yet younger selves conceive
here's music's music and the day of day

are worlds collapsing?any was a glove
but i'm and you are actual either hand
is when for sale?forever is to give
and on forever's very now we stand

nor a first rose explodes but shall increase
whole truthful infinite immediate us

A SELECTED LIST OF TITLES IN THE
Universal Library

LITERATURE, CRITICISM, DRAMA, AND POETRY

PSYCHOLOGY

OTHER TITLES OF INTEREST

THE TASTEMAKERS

By

RUSSELL LYNES

"TASTE," *says the author of this book, "is our personal pleasure, our private dilemma and our public facade.*" THE TASTEMAKERS *is the lively story of the people and pressures that have shaped American taste for the last dozen decades.*

In a serious but witty and perceptive account, Mr. Lynes gives the battles of the tastemakers the dignity or humor they deserve — battles that are sometimes solemn and full of conviction, sometimes pompous, sometimes gay and frivolous. He reanimates — with all their original intensity and excitement — the battles of taste that account for our likes and dislikes today.

"It is a highly original job, very sound in scholarship, very sagacious, and constantly amusing. ...The way he lightly transforms himself into an encyclopedia of American culture is delightful and a little breathtaking." BERNARD DEVOTO

"It reads like the liveliest conversation of a wise friend—the sort of conversation one always wishes would find its way into a book." HERBERT AGAR

UL-54

WITH NAPOLEON IN RUSSIA

By

ARMAND DE CAULAINCOURT

In August, *1933, an architect looking among the ruins of General Armand de Caulaincourt's old chateau in Picardy, noticed a battered iron chest in a pile of debris. On opening the chest he discovered the long-lost original manuscript of General de Caulaincourt's fabulous memoirs. Upon study, these memoirs turned out to be the most important discovery of Napoleonic materials in our time, for in them was a complete eye-witness account of how the Emperor planned and fought his greatest and most disastrous war—his invasion of Russia.*

No book on Napoleon has more bearing on the events of today than this astounding chronicle of the struggle between the Emperor and the Czar. Here is revealed not only the thoughts and actions of the great Emperor as recorded by his most distinguished aide and confidant, but also startling insights into the enigmatic character and ways of the Russians, whom Caulaincourt knew well since he had been Ambassador to the court of St. Petersburg.

Scholars and students will find fascinating parallels in the events of then and now. They will also find within these pages the most vivid closeup of Napoleon that we possess, the picture of a man considered a deity by many, possessed of the most remarkable qualities of leadership, yet prisoner of irrational obsessions that led him to defeat.

UL-55

MADAME BOVARY

BY

GUSTAVE FLAUBERT

MADAME BOVARY *has been called the first modern novel. Its influence on subsequent writers has been profound enough to warrant that description. Flaubert's magnificent achievement was to present a perfect perception of his characters with perfect objectivity. The result in* MADAME BOVARY *was a new kind of realism that shocked its first readers to the core. It remains for readers today just as impressive an experience. The tragedy of Emma Bovary is inexorable and belongs to the grand tradition of tragedy, but it is peculiarly modern, too. There is no appeal to the gods or to fate, no suggestion of a deus ex machina, however disguised. Step by step, with every action and motivation almost frighteningly real, Emma makes her own tragedy—and every other character is equally fully conceived. It is as if Flaubert had created whole people rather than characters of fiction and had then abandoned them to work out their own lives. But a closer examination reveals that this impression is achieved only through the most exquisitely painstaking craft.*

UL-57

NINE PLAYS OF CHEKOV

THE *delicate capture of a passing mood, the keen sympathy with the Hamlet in all human beings, the poignant probing of an overwhelming frustration—these are the elements which make up Chekov's dramatic vision of life. These plays of the twilight make Chekov, to the Russia of today, perhaps more alien than any other writer of the first rank, though he has been a major influence upon dramatists of the West.*

Perhaps Chekov's basic contribution to the stage can be summed up in the statement that he de-theatricalized the theatre. His plays end, as T. S. Eliot might say, not with a bang but a whimper. He demonstrates that tragedy can be as real in the slow wasting away of lives as in the great dramas of fore-destined catastrophe. He deals with human fate in a minor key.

That Chekov's dramas are of enduring appeal is proven by repeated revivals of his works. This volume, containing four of his major plays and five one-act masterpieces, also provides a valuable chronological table of the playwright's life and works.   UL-59

THE ART OF LOVE

AND OTHER LOVE BOOKS OF

OVID

Ovid's ART OF LOVE *has been called, in the words of the* Encyclopaedia Britannica, *"perhaps the most immoral book ever written by a man of genius." Its erotic brilliance appealed to the prevailing taste of the fashionable world of Ovid's day, an era of gross moral laxity, and has continued to fascinate readers for nearly 2000 years.*

Written in the elegant and graceful language of sophisticated Augustan Rome, the first two books of the ART OF LOVE *contain advice for the predatory male. The third book is devoted to aiding the female in her pursuit of the male. All three books are cast in the conventional form of the erotic Alexandrian elegy, but are graced with Ovid's unique wit.*

This volume also contains Ovid's other love books: THE LOVES, *in which he wrote about his mistress Corinna;* LOVE'S CURE, *a prescription for falling out of love; and* THE ART OF BEAUTY, *some further advice to the fair sex.*

It is interesting to note that of all the ancient poets, it was Ovid who made the most powerful impression on such writers as Marlowe, Spenser, Shakespeare, Milton and Dryden.   UL-61

CRIME AND PUNISHMENT

By

FYODOR DOSTOEVSKY

IT WOULD *probably be appalling to count the number of intelligent readers who have been put off from reading* Crime and Punishment *by its curious reputation as a classic of gloom — both classic and gloominess somehow suggest dullness. Nothing could be farther from Dostoevsky's masterpiece than the suggestion of dullness — disturbing, yes, even terrifying, but* Crime and Punishment *is more thrilling than any novel ever written to provide thrills.*

As Dorothy Brewster says in the introduction to this edition: "The plot, simple enough in outline, is full of breathless suspense and hair-raising episodes. It may be taken quite naively as one of the most thrilling of detective stories. Or just as naively — but more solemnly — as a Christian drama of sin and retribution…or into it may be read psychological, philosophical, and even metaphysical significance, to the limit of one's capacity for such speculation. On whatever levels of response it touches the reader's imagination, it is certain to be a disturbing experience."   UL-63